The Joy of Painting
Alma Redlinger

100 years since the birth of the painter

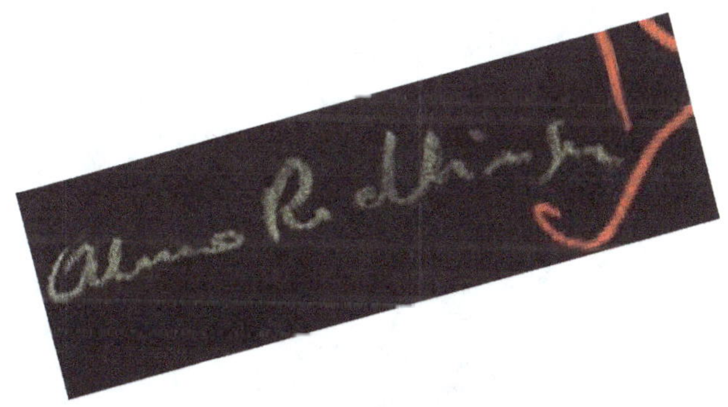

The Joy of Painting

Alma Redlinger

Sources: Internet - Daria Simion - Vasile Petrovici

Tehno and translation - Adrian Grauenfels

Thanks to Mrs. Daria Simion for the kind guidance and the reproductions that appear in the book.

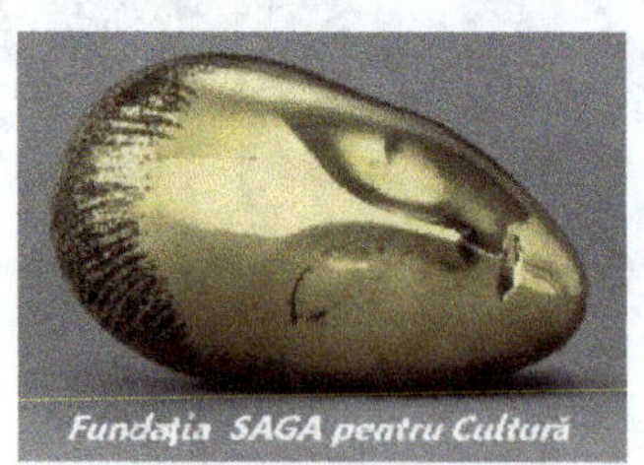

SAGA Foundation for Culture - 2024

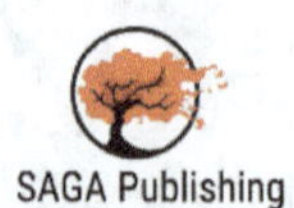

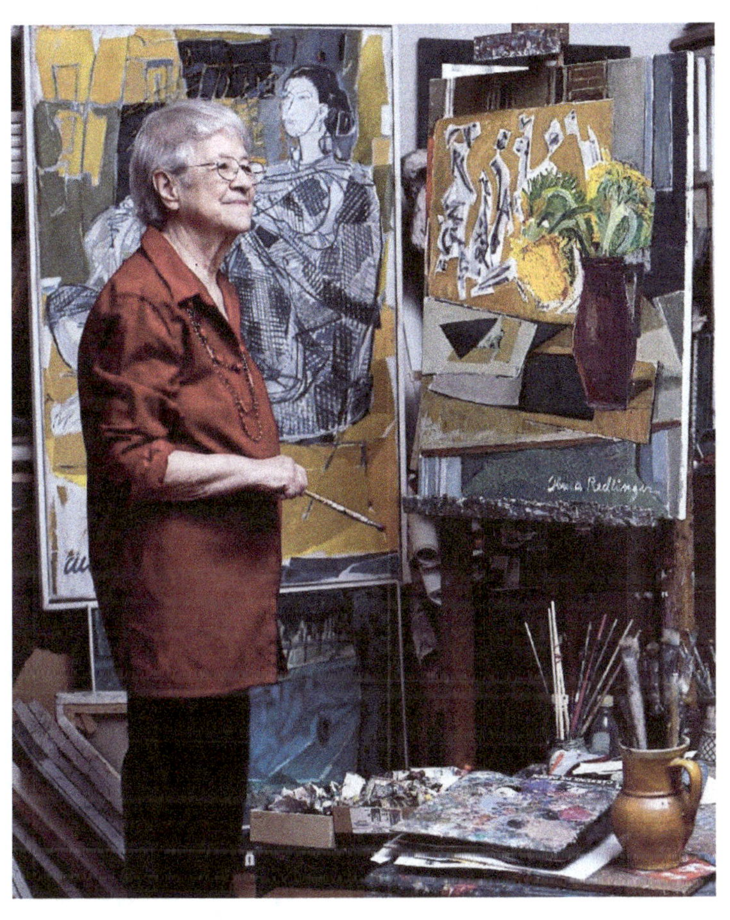

Contents

A short biography

100 years ago Alma was born in Bucharest - Romania:

"Alma Redlinger built from the beginning a career that was avant-garde in its essence. The artist's work is of high value, shows exceptional coherence, and is an example for those who have chosen art as their life's destiny. Alma Redlinger belongs to the generation of artists who ensure the continuity between inter-war and contemporary painting." (Octavian BARBOSA, 1976)

About ALMA

8 March 1924 -2 February 2017, Bucharest

Studies: Free Academy of Painting at the School of Arts for Jews (1940-1944) and Guguianu Free Academy (1944-1945), teacher painter M. H. Maxy

Married to Ladislau Redlinger, in 1944, they have two daughters, Ileana and Daria.

Since 1945 she has participated in all the official state, municipal, and republican salons, including some organized in the provinces, of painting and graphics. He also took part in group exhibitions in the country and abroad. She also works and participates in exhibitions of decorative art and small tapestry and illustrates several books.

Her works on two frescoes: in 1959-1961, the monumental work "Folk Dances" at the Poiana Brasov sports complex, in collaboration with Mimi Şaraga Maxy, and 1963-1964, the monumental work "Pioneers", fresco and mosaic, on the façade of the school at 122 Antim Street in Bucharest (school demolished in the eighties when Ceauşescu started building the People's House. The school was located next to Antim church. The church was moved).

27 PERSONAL EXHIBITIONS - in Bucharest and the country

5 EXHIBITIONS IN MEMORIAM: 2017 at ICR Vienna, 2018 at ICR Bucharest, 2018 at Simeza Gallery, 2023 National Museum of Contemporary Art, 2024 Art Safari.

 Her works are in museums and collections in Romania (MNAR, MNAC, Visual Art Museum Galați, Municipal Library "Radu Rosetti" Onești, National Art Museum Bacău, Bucovinei Museum Suceava, etc.),

France, Italy, Germany, Israel (Marcel Iancu Museum, Ein Hod), USA, Japan, Brazil, Netherlands, Canada, Belgium, Greece, England, Sweden, (...)

AWARDS: "Simu" prize for youth - 1945, Ministry of Arts prize - 1946, 3rd prize at the World Youth Festival - Moscow - 1953, member of the "Academia Italia delle Arti e del'Lavoro" - 1980, awarded the Academy's gold medal - 1981 and the "Oscar d'Italia" - 1985, Order of Cultural Merit in the rank of Commander - 2004, Nomination for the Margareta Sterian Prize - 2005, "Marcel Iancu" Prize for Fine Arts - 2006, "Nihil Sine Deo" Decoration - awarded by HM King Michael I - 2011, Nomination for the "Nihil Sine Deo" Decoration - awarded by HM King Michael I - 2011, Nomination for the "Nihil Sine Deo" Decoration - awarded by HM King Michael I - 2011, Nomination for the "Marcel Iancu" Prize for

Fine Arts - 2006. Prometheus Opera Omnia" by Anonimul Foundation - 2011.

Some of the most important books and albums of his work: 2009, "Alma Redlinger, painting until 2009", authors Vasile Petrovici and Daria Simion, ALEXIS publishing house, coordinating director Mihai Vişinescu who opened the series of art albums "Contemporary Romanian Plastic Artists"; 2011, the album of the exhibition at Sala Dalles by Adrian Buga published by UNARTE publishing house; 2014, "Talking with Alma Redlinger" by Vasile Petrovici, Corint Educational Publishing House, Coresi; 2014, the exhibition album "90 years of life, 70 years of painting" by Adrian Buga;

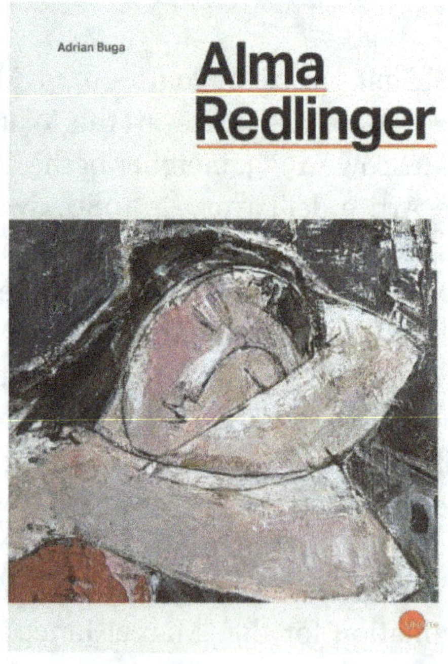

"Alma Redlinger's paintings and drawings are based on the system, the rigor imposed by reason. A strong drawing, with broken planes and firm lines, builds 2015, "Alma Redlinger - graphics" by Ileana Redlinger and Daria Simion, CNI CORESI Publishing House; 2016, the exhibition album "The Island" by Ileana Redlinger and Daria Simion, published by Conceptual Gallery; and others. the composition. The gesture is quick, sure, and capable of drawing out the essence, of discovering the optimal position of each thing under analysis. It is surprising how, over the years, in this continuous dialogue between line and splash of color, Alma Redlinger has been able to harmonize the cold gaze with the emotional power of perception. The charm of her pictoriality is to be found in this dialogue that she knows how to make the most of the diverse possibilities of plastic expression. It is a gentle confrontation between the severity construction and color, between lucid analysis and the particular moment of perception. The individuality of Alma Redlinger's creation is found in this subtle, balanced play between drawing and color, in the very special sonority of her chromatics, and the rhythm of her compositions, which develop a strong inner force.

Alma Redlinger's style is energetic and rigorous. The artist controls the surface of the painting down to the last detail, attentive to the expressive variety, to the composition of the objects, concerned with conveying the mood, the feeling of a moment. This explains the great variety of this painting in the context of relatively restricted subjects. The painter's favourite subjects come from the familiar environment; the studio, people nearby, family or friends, and the objects around her allow her to continually create other compositions or still lifes. With these "props," she has built her work over more than fifty years. The freshness of her work comes from her ability to record that special moment, the new light in which she sees an old object, the charm of a flower, and the way things around her are composed. Most images are from her studio, in some compositions she depicts corners or broad images of the loom, in others she restricts herself to a few objects or books, but everything is viewed so that the human presence exists. (...)

"The sincerity of Alma Redlinger's discourse is captivating. Her painting is not only believable but, I would say, even beneficial, in its ability to convey to the viewer the joy of the moment and a new, reconsidered image of the universe in whose intimacy we live."

Alma Redlinger - Atelier, 2006, CULTURAL OBSERVER Maria-Magdalena CRISAN

**

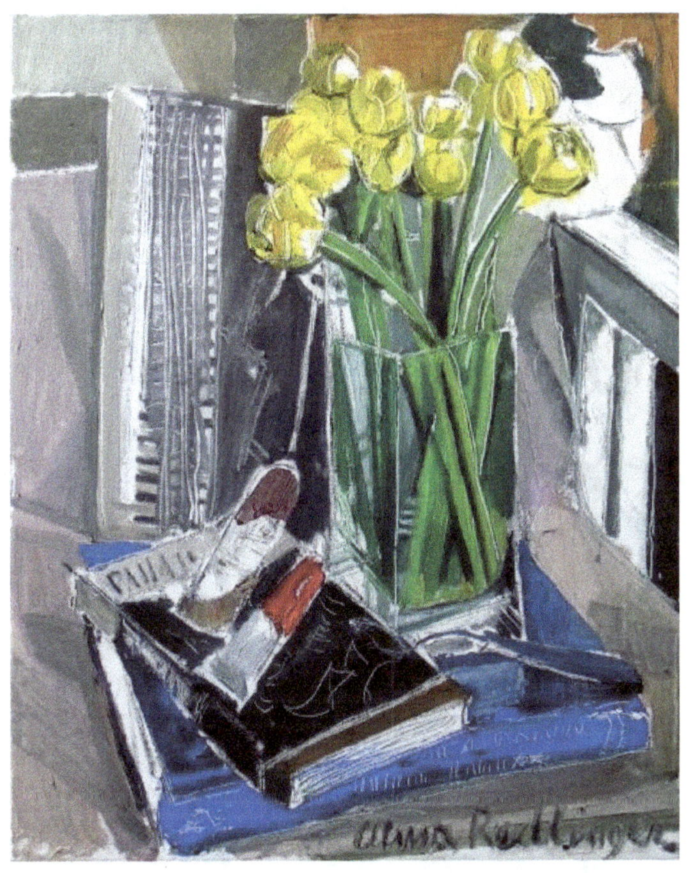

Yellow water lilies with Theodor Palladi album, 2011, 55 × 45 cm

Thanks to the kind permission of Alma's daughter, Mrs. Daria Simion, I had access to the text "Talking to Alma Redlinger" by the collector Vasile Petrovici. An interesting biography constructed from conversations with the artist and her husband and daughters. We have cut out a series of dialogues that shed light on our artist.

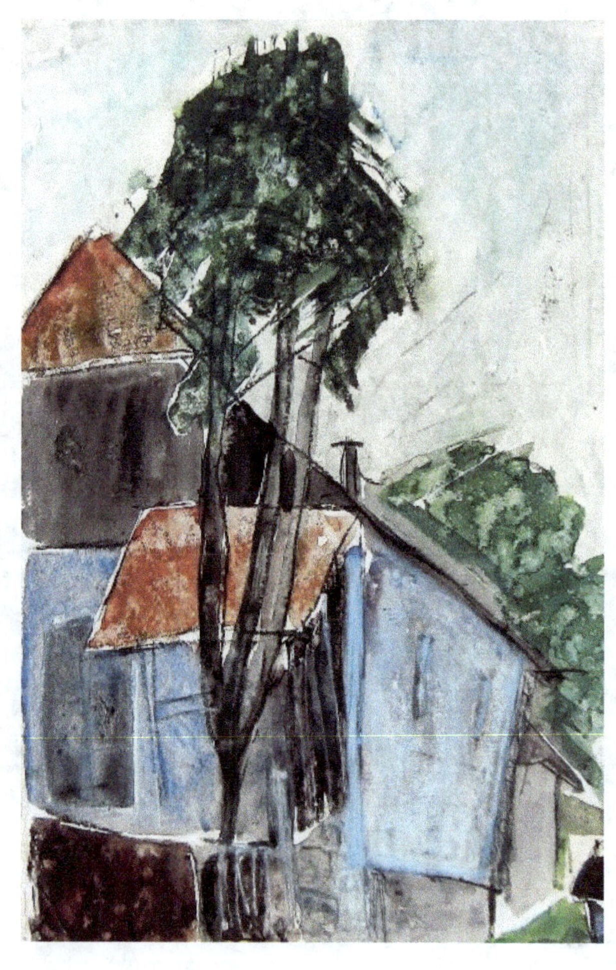

Tree with Blue House, 1980, watercolor,
49.5 × 33.5 cm

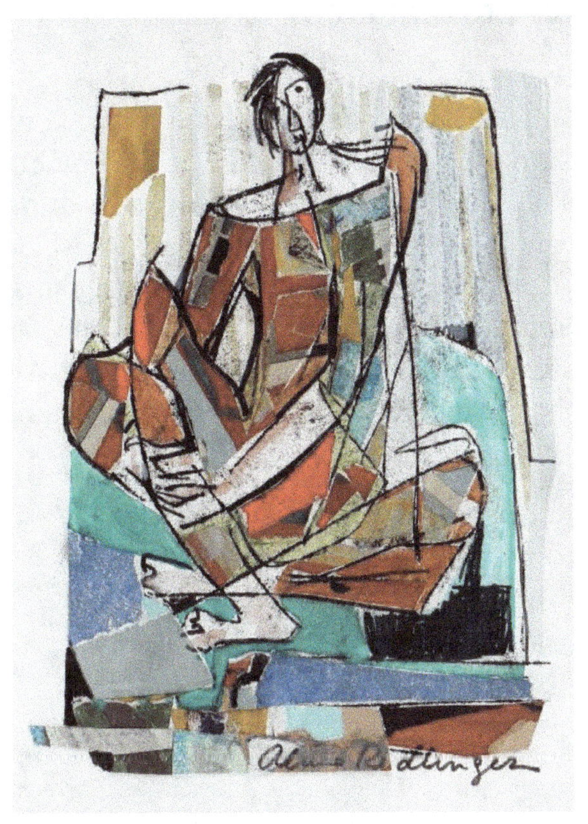

del

in the studio, mixed media

A short presentation

"...When she was sixteen she came to the house of her future in-laws, in the middle of the bombing of Bucharest. She enrolled at the Maxy school, where she received her first notions about art - to which she would always remain faithful. She worships her teacher and cherishes her classmates. The studio is always at home, in the bosom of the family. After a while, her own home looks like a little museum,

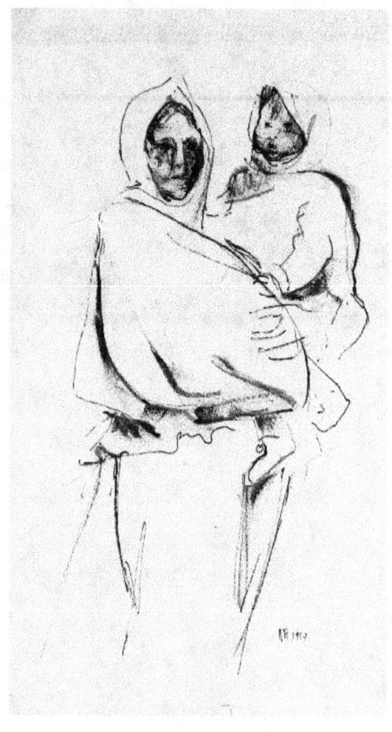

Maternity, 1957, ink/paper, 22 ×15 cm

decorated with paintings. She participates in documentaries and creative camps, often in the company of her good friend Eva Cerbu, with whom she has many ties, in art and life.

She travels extensively, usually with her husband Laci, and Ladislau Redlinger. On these trips, she mostly makes drawings and sketches, which she develops on her return home into large compositions on canvas. She values her friends, artists, and art critics.

Alma Redlinger is dedicated to her work, she feels "the joy of painting", and she has admirers on several continents. Some of them, consistent in their love, become true collectors of the artist.

Photographs and reproductions occupy an important place in the economy of the book. They support the dialogue and come, for the most part, from the Redlinger family archive. A smaller part of them is my contribution. Their arrangement on the page is the fruit of the work and good inspiration of Mrs Alma's daughter, Daria Simion."

Vasile PETROVICI, 2014, Modernism.ro

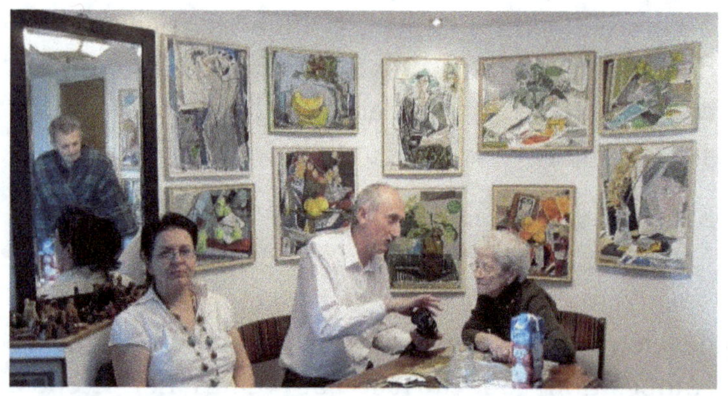

Florica and Vasile Petrovici with Alma Redlinger,
2013

Alma about their home

"Through the window, you can see, far away, the block on Nicolae Bălcescu Boulevard, with the house you know so well... if the block hadn't had a "red bulb", with all the noise and pollution in the "belly of Bucharest", we wouldn't have moved. The place was spacious, the workshop very bright... I think you can feel it in my works there, they have more light and more color. We were a stone's throw from exhibitions, museums... I didn't miss a single opening. I was close to the George Enescu Square of the Athenaeum where I went to the musical evenings during the Enescu festival... cinemas, theatres... I was very attached to this house. It was hard for me to leave there... but it was just as hard to leave all the homes I've lived in over the seventy years I've been with Laci..."

About her Parents

"My father (Marcu Polacu), was born on March 29, 1889, in Câmpeni, district of Moineşti, and died on September 17, 1965, in Bucharest. I have no record of his profession, but I know that he was engaged in the forestry business. After 23 August he was a dogar worker. With all his re-qualification as a worker, the regime sent him to prison. Sorin, my nephew, on behalf of my sister Nectara, tells of his dignity and humanity: when he returned home, weak as a bull and without any income, he took care to send him, on Palas Street, to a lady whose husband was still in prison, with potatoes, cabbage, and bread. She made that journey until her husband returned home. Every autumn she made must. From time to time she told of her time with the cavalry regiment in the Balkan War of 1913 for which she received a brevet and decoration from King Ferdinand.

My mother (Lora Polacu), Lora Leibu by her maiden name, was born on January 5, 1895, in the commune of Poduri, district of Moineşti, and died on November 30, 1972, in Bucharest.

Their marriage took place on August 5, 1912, also in Poduri commune, Moinești district. They had 5 children, two of whom died. They were all born in Poduri, only I was born in Bucharest. My mother was a housewife all her life. Although she didn't go to high school, she had the gift of reading. She especially liked the river novels, Forsyte Saga, Henry IV... She was an extraordinary cook! She had the pleasure of cooking at any celebration. On Jewish holidays she would make a stuffed pike, varenikes (tusks stuffed with goose liver), and Passover hummus. At Christmas, she made sarmas and muffins. There was a great love between my parents... I keep a picture from their wedding, my mother in a wedding dress and my father in a tuxedo with a white bow tie. Mom sometimes told stories about her life at the Bridges when she had a carriage and Dad was a businessman. Sorin remembers her as a small and loving girl. She says he's glad that "the little mouth" caught his marriage to Petronela a few months before she died. And Petronela, even now after all these years, remembers that "buțica" warned her that it wouldn't be easy with him, to which Sorin replies that grandparents are always right, having more life experience! That's what the children used to call their grandparents: 'buțu' and 'buțica'."

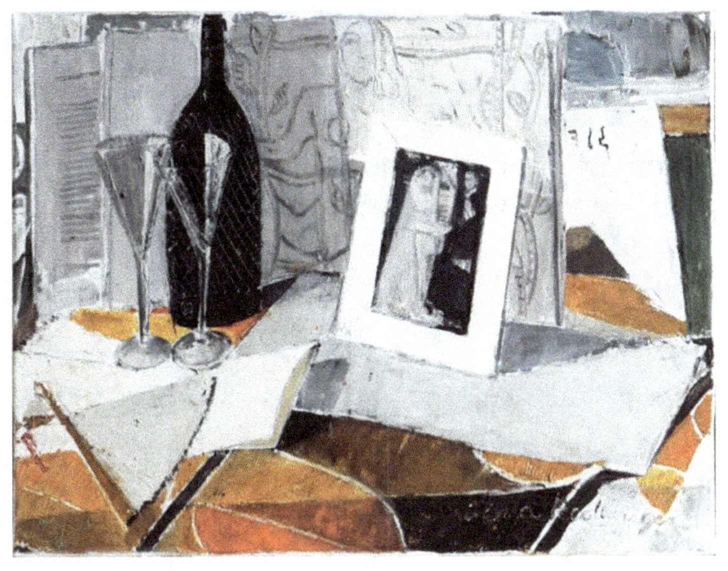

The bride and groom of the 1920s, 2008,
60 × 80 cm

About family and school

"Family was my first school, the bond of a lifetime and many lifetimes, the nest from which I flew, to build my next nests, the trajectory of passage from past to present and future, the security of tomorrow and the basis of survival... Warmth and peace for creation, love and tenderness, trust and hope, the joy of being with loved ones every day... for me, for us, family has always been very important.

I graduated from the elementary school "Regina Maria". During my first year of high school, I worked at the "Ştirbei" girls' high school, my second year at the "Domniţa Ileana" girls' high school, and I continued at the "Domniţa Bălaşa" high commercial school which was a *During* commercial school. I didn't take the ability exam, racial laws were already imposed excluding Jews from schools.

(...)

Aunt Fani, who lived with us, helped me when she found out about Maxy's school. I had a certain inclination towards drawing. I got good marks in school for my dexterities, including drawing. Fani got interested and took me there, I auditioned, and Maxy thought I could start, and see how it went. I started - and stayed there for four years while I was at school (1940-1944). I started when I was sixteen.

There were about nine of us students, more or less at different times. There were three of us who were permanent: me,

Marius Coppelman and the future director Lucian Bratu, then called Bergman. There were always others who came and stayed for a while, then left. For example, Dorel Pascal was there for a while, the future architect and professor Mihail Caffé, we call him Toto, and the future poet and writer Nina Cassian...

That's how I found my way. It was a chance. Another colleague, Lica

Roman, went to Paris. She came to classes less often. Yvonne Hasan spent some time at Maxy and became an upholsterer and teacher at the Institute. Maria Constantin (Mița) became a watercolorist. Maxy also taught at a school, the Technical and Artistic University. Eva Cerbu also studied there. Interestingly, Eva, Mița, and Yvonne took, after 1948, some courses in plastic studies with Alexandru Ciucurencu at the Institute of Plastic Arts "Nicolae Grigorescu" in Bucharest. I did not attend those courses.

Eva and I exhibited together at the Maxy School. In the first trips, and documentaries we were together. We got closer and we became friends for life. Maxy's studio was in the Jewish Art School. At the "Art School for Jews", M.H. Maxy ran the painting section, Beate Fredanov the drama section, and Alfred Mendelsohn the music section. There was also the "Marcu Onescu" College for Social Sciences; the college headed by engineer Ernest Abason for exact sciences. Maxy was also a teacher at Abason's college. After four years at Maxy's school, I studied another year at the Guguianu Free Academy, on Polizu Street, opposite the Polytechnic. Here I was a classmate of Eva Cerbu, Spiru Chintilă, Constantin Berdilă, Mimi Șaraga, and others. Maxy was also our teacher.

The program was like this: we did one paper a week. We worked according to the model we brought and we paid for it. For example, the actor Sandu Sticlaru was one of

our models. Some funny things happened. We found an old man on the street whom we brought into the studio and paid him every day. I paid him, the old man was unshaven, unkempt, untidy. The next day he came in shaved and tidied up. He ruined our picture. Wednesday Maxy was coming in to correct. He'd go round to each one. Sometimes he'd even draw us a picture of the pattern. I've got one of those. Saturday was the critique. All the drawings were put up on the wall, and we'd comment on what was good and what wasn't. And at these critiques, there were guests, for example, Titina Călugăru, Mendelsohn... Maxy's acquaintances.

(...)

It was important to critique the works. I learned a lot from the concrete discussions of my work and that of my colleagues. Something else was important: Maxy also guided us in theoretical education, and art history, and introduced us to all European and universal art. He gave us homework, for example on impressionism. One week we did impressionism, one week we did constructivism, and we went through all the "isms", so to speak. I worked a lot on drawing with Maxy. He said that painting should be based on drawing. We didn't work from the model. He would introduce us theoretically, show us pictures of works by artists in different styles, discuss them with us, and follow the work in that style. I have a work of mine from school with an attempt at cubist style. He was passionate.

Each lesson also meant extensive expositions on the work of important painters, introducing us to the history of classical and modern, Romanian and universal art."

About Drawing

"Most of the time I did drawing. From the beginning, I worked according to the model. I learned about composition and aesthetic principles, and maybe that's when I learned to convey an atmosphere, a character, a feeling.

The color I studied for about a year and a half towards the end.

In fact, in pencil and charcoal drawing we had also learned to enhance, to render patterns in shades of grey, to highlight the drawing with the tension between light and shadow, to put accents that bring out contrasts, a whole technique... Color brought us joy, we took a step forward...

A characteristic of Professor Maxy was that each student developed their skills and talent, each went their own way but all learned that at the heart of painting is drawing, construction, and composition. And very importantly: most of them went on to become established painters with distinct personalities. Maxy has passed this passion on to us for life!

It created a collegial atmosphere of competition and curiosity. Maxy had charisma, he was an exceptional teacher. We were lucky.

Laci intervenes - Don't forget that we were generally all young and very young, at the questionable age of personality formation, of maturation, and there was something else, the many political tensions, the war, the anti-Jewish state laws... All of this made us look for a way in life. School lasted around three hours a day because most of the day, Jews were forced to go to "compulsory work", in work detachments but also to "statistics" where girls went too, from 1940 until 1944. I did compulsory labor in different places in Bucharest: Vama Obor, the Institute of Statistics, the mills on Ștefan cel Mare road, Colentina hospital, Cișmigiu area..."

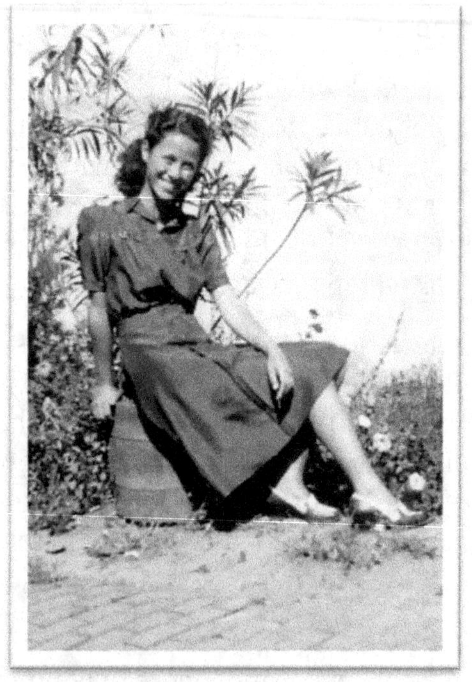

Alma Polak

About Colleagues

"I had many colleagues, some for a longer or shorter time: Pita Rubin, Lelia Zuaf David, Linica Siegler-Els, Wilma Badian, Tia Peltz, Dorio Lazăr, Mihai (Danu) Leibovici, Sonia Natra, Valerica Leibovici, brothers Emma and Sergiu Mishosniky. I was recently visited by their granddaughter Lala Mishosniky who also sent me a portrait I made in 1942 of Sergiu's wife.

Anca Arghir was also my colleague. She became a publicist and wrote art reviews and essays. She now lives in Germany. I also had colleagues Puiu Wechsler, Toto Caffé, Eva Munteanu."

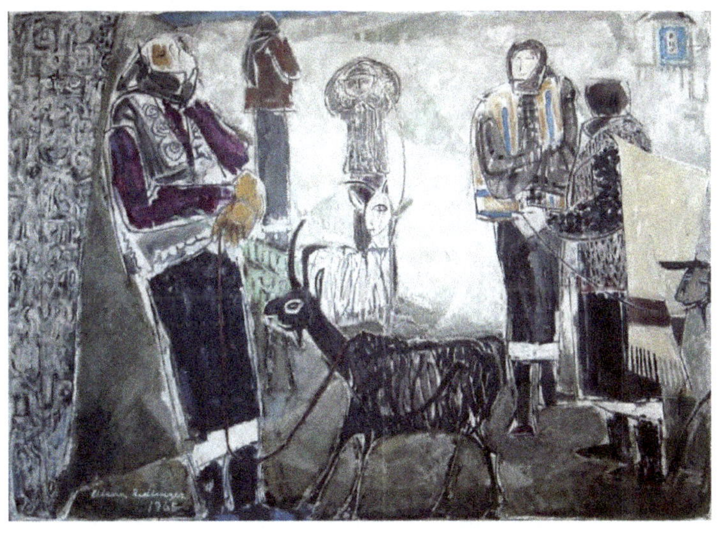

The goat fair at Pătârlagele, 1965, 135 × 200 cm

The Painting Studio

"Atelier? I worked in a room in the house. In Iuliu Tetrat Street I had a room where I lived and worked. It was a small but bright room. Around 1944. After the war. After that, we moved to Pangrati on the corner of Zambaccian. I lived with my husband's family until I was 28.

 In my first years after school, I worked on landscapes, still, I have an oil painting of Mitropolia Hill, with an urban landscape seen from above. I also worked according to the model. Of course, some works stayed with friends, and family, others "left", it's hard to remember... many drawings I still have.

 In those days the Union gave loans and if I wanted another loan I had to pay off the loan beforehand. And I used to make all kinds of things that I gave to the Plastic Fund: little markers, greeting cards, prints, different ornaments and that's how I paid off my loan. This work took a lot of my time away from painting and I didn't have much time left for housework either.

 For painting, you needed canvases, colors, and brushes. In addition, there was the documentation for which I received materials for painting. Of course, it was also a help for the family.

Daria - *The apartment on the ground floor, on Zoe Alley, was designed for a painter. The studio was on the north side, it had zenithal light, and it had quite a big balcony. We had neighbors the Moldoveanu family and later the family of Dr. Arh.*

Radu Patrulius who was my professor at the Faculty of Architecture.

In Zoe Alley, the studio was quite big and bright, on

one wall was an oval mirror and I made a work with the studio and the mirror, reproduced in the album "Alma Redlinger", made with Daria. I gave it to Nina Cassian. I was sorry when I left that studio, it was my best studio...

The apartment was bought by a family through intimidation and we found out after the transaction. Then we moved to Haga Street. The workshop in Haga Street was not big but we had enough space and a nice atmosphere for work. I had a Linden tree by the windows that shaded me. I made a painting, "Bucharest Autumn", in which you can see the houses across the street and the lime tree in the window. The Dorobanți neighborhood, where I lived for many years, is one of the most beautiful neighborhoods in Bucharest.

 I didn't leave Haga Street willingly either, a landlord appeared! When we found the house in Bălcescu, we were happy with our fate. Alma reorganized the workshop and soon started working. Yes, I felt good in the workshop in Balcescu. I had good light in the morning, the studio was on the west side, and in the afternoon it was harder to work, the sun drove me away in the corners without shadows. In Bălcescu the rooms were high and there I had space to expose up to the top. And it was very good. Here we were restricted, but still as much as I could put on the walls I did. I put them up because I enjoy seeing them. In fact, in all the apartments we had as much work on the walls as we could fit. It's the same with my daughter Ileana and my grandson Stefan and it was the same with my sister Nectara.

(...)

I had the chance to be able to work at home, to be near Laci and the children, I had the chance that Laci not only understood me and supported me in my work but also admired me.

Daria - *All of Alma's workshops were for us full of mystery, a fantasy world, full of imagination. When we were children we hardly dared to enter the studio, later on, our mother would finish a work and we would start arguing about the painting: it's mine! it's mine! Stefan, when he was very young, used to enter the studio and wanted to compete with Pica, and now Tudor, not even five years old, asked one day: "Does Pica still have a painting?*

does he still need this painting?" or even try a collaboration with Pica. We find him fingering the painting which is leaning against the table on the floor and not yet dry...

Laci - A poem about the workshop

"The workshop is

the environment, the laboratory where sketches are worked on,

impressions, the connection to the world, everyday life, work

uninterrupted work, the pleasure of living, the perpetual school...

The workshop is

the place where tradition meets and combines with the new,

where long contemplation overlaps

spontaneity, where one returns again and again to what began and never completed...

The workshop is

like a permanent museum where canvases and drawings are

colors invade you, and the shapes of much more
 then a few unknown ones are born...

The workshop is

home, the window to the world, the place where you are never

alone, where you meet the boundlessness, the time without beginning and without end...

The workshop is

the present, the place from where you start towards exhibitions and where you

return to continue and start again..."

Documentary travel

"VP. Were there lots of places to document across the country?

AR Yes. We would choose where we wanted to go.

Ileana Redlinger: My mother and Eva had a saying: "la noi la Bacău", or "la noi la Focşani". All the places they went to became familiar, known... on some sketches of men or women their names and village or address were written. They made friends with the locals. They also went to Turia in the area of Târgului Secuiesc, Nehoiu with the surrounding villages, among which Pătârlagele where the painting "Târgul de capre de la Pătârlagele" appeared, Năruja near Focşani, Târgovişte, Galaţi, Târgul Jiu, Baia Mare, Bacău, Giurgiu, Lenauheim, Brăila, at Tescani, in some places they were several times, for example at Reşiţa, at Deva, at Sarmisegetuza, and of course in the neighborhoods of Bucharest and the surrounding fairs.

(...)

In August 1973, Eva and I went to Giurgiu with a group of twelve people. I was about to be arrested because to some militiamen I seemed "suspicious". We often had such adventures with local officials: in the 1965 documentation, in Nehoiu, one day at a fair we sat down to draw and were interrupted by a militiaman who asked us for our documents because the curious people who had gathered around us were disturbing the onion trade of a small market girl and she had called the militiaman. After he had written a whole polylogue with all the details of the service order and the bulletin he left us alone and we could go about our work."

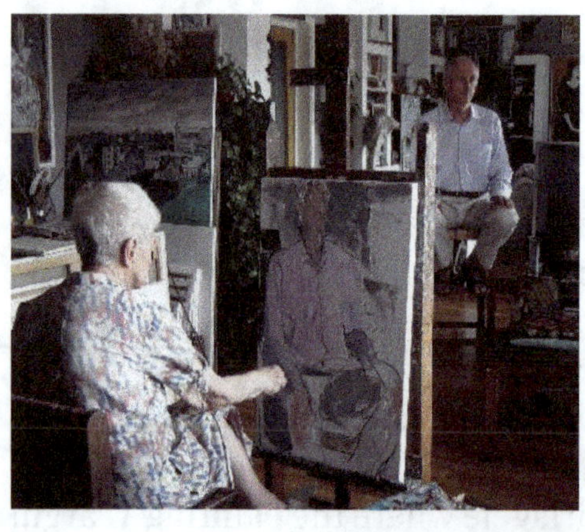

Portrait of the Collector Vasile Petrovici, 2013, 80 × 50 cm

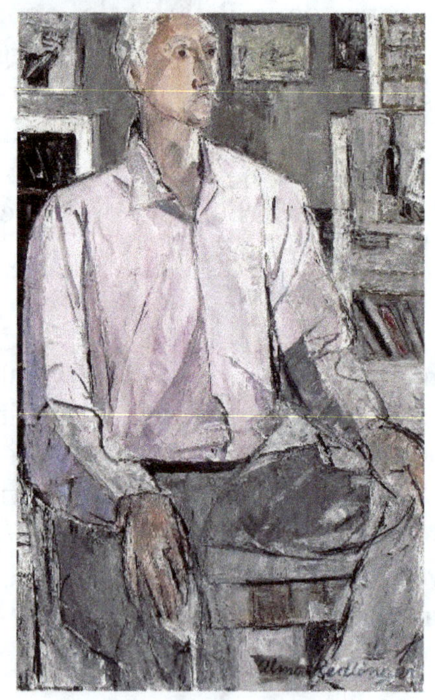

Subjects

"Portrait. Landscape. I also did the landscape. I did a painting, which was also exhibited at the Dalles, called "On the Constanta Bridge".

 I sat there on the Constanta Bridge and painted. I had no problems with people coming and looking. In Carol Park, I did paintings and landscapes. By the sea. When I don't have a subject that "pulls" me, I arrange different interior themes: a few objects, flowers, or something else. Or I do self-portraits."

From large to small

"VP -When did your canvases get smaller? You did large canvases at first and then they got smaller.

AR- I've also done large works in the last few houses, I also do them.

I'm still doing them now. I used to do large works when there were Official Shows. If you showed a small work, it was either seen or not seen. They put it in a corner. On the side. On the other hand, there were papers based on papers on certain subjects. The topics were given in a general way, for example, topics in industry, topics in agriculture, and topics for an anniversary. They were compositions that required space. As there were no more Official

Salons, the dimensions were reduced, but I like to work on a large scale.

I recently did a work with the album "Gheorghe Petraşcu" by Eleonora Costescu, open to Lucretia's portrait. Petraşcu also did smaller works."

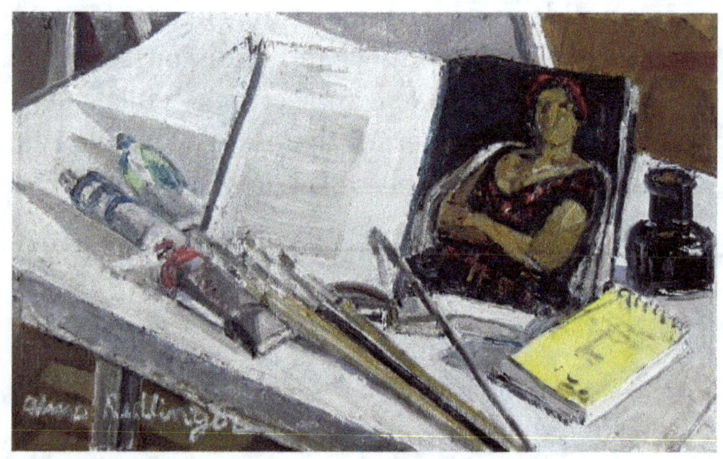

Petraşcu Album, 2012, 30 × 50 cm

Working techniques

"The drawings, the compositions I do in monotype. And then I make a combination of colors in collage with various materials or papers that I paint in different colors and that I match, so to speak. After these collages, many times, I made paintings, because I liked the harmony and the drawing and I passed it on to painting. It's happened the other way around too.

LR - The collages he does like this: he prints about ten to twenty papers and then goes to the second phase for all of them. Then he goes to the third phase, finishing. Each of the twenty is another drawing. Sometimes he repeats the same sketch (with the same subject) but in the end, it's a different work. For example after 'Woman with the Green Hat' came 'Woman with the Red Hat' and 'Woman with the Agate Hat'."

Flowers

"I painted all kinds of flowers, even sunflowers and peonies and "de Brebu" roses but my favorite flowers were magnolias, yellow honeysuckles, field flowers, scapes of all kinds, dandelions, maples, but also chestnuts, I also painted forsias, even a bonsai, and all kinds of branches and leaves. The girls bring them to me every year and they inspire me almost every time.

Many times I've made color ranges, "played" on paper, on holidays, and in moments of break from work. I have sketchbooks and cartoons, full of such color studies, compositions of shapes, and a search for balance between form, color, light, and contrast. Today I often use them as background in interior themes. They are a combination of concrete and abstract.

When I design an interior theme I start from a construction, a range of colours. I have often painted books in the background, I even painted a "Tower of Babel" of books, it was called "Books in the Workshop", the work is at Diana Teitler, a collector of my work. I have many works in which I used albums, catalogs, or even posters of Romanian or foreign artists. They compose very well and create cultural analogies

Self-portraits

Daria- The last self-portrait, the one from 2011 that was exhibited with Rembrandt's classic 1954 "Self-Portrait" in the chiaroscuro technique at the Veroniki Art "Atelier 2011" in early 2012, has a whole story:

...on a winter's day, with the radiators hot, I see my mother in her fur coat buttoned up tight, sitting with a mirror on the easel and sketchbook in hand working on a self-portrait! In front of her leaning on the bookcase and the bundle of canvases: Self-Portrait 1954. She tried the new portrait with a beret, and a straw hat, and eventually after a few days she was left with only a plug around her neck and her house dress. (...)

AR - The two self-portraits at 30 and 87 years of age were giving each other a replica over time, they were the focus of the exhibition and the interviews taken. I was wondering where this last painting came from. The self-portrait at 30 is in our room. For every exhibition I do a self-portrait, I thought I'd do a replica so to speak. Luiza Barcan asked me how I feel now when I put the two self-portraits together. a man's life... a man's life and daily work... not much has changed, only the brush I replaced with the painting knife...

(...)

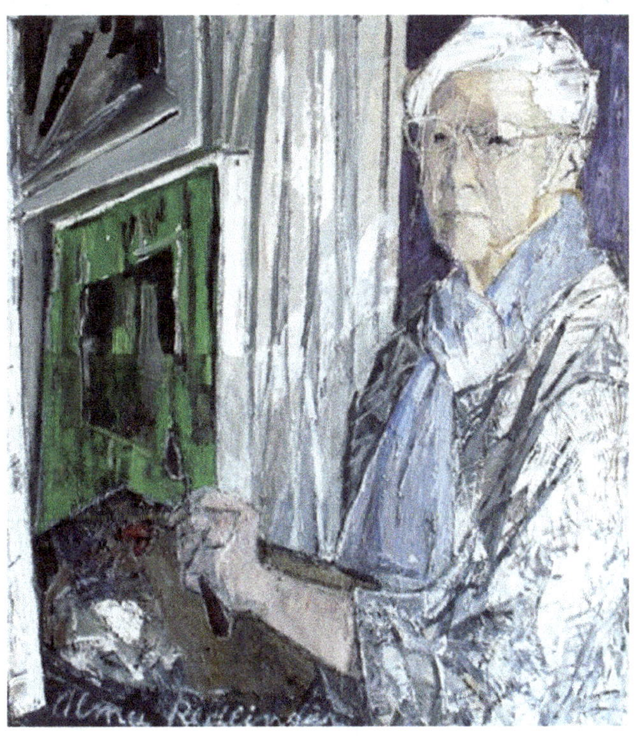

Self-portrait, 2011, 55 × 50 cm

I've seen that Ana also has some self-portraits, very good, it's very good. I advise young artists to do self-portraits. It's a dialogue between the present and the future with becoming an artist. I have painted Arina Gheorghiță several times, she's a good model, a great model, so why not be a good model for her? As far as I know, she has not done self-portraits. (...)

Sometimes I also used the "picture-in-picture technique". In a way it came by itself... the studio was always full of my paintings, and albums, but also postcards with reproductions of works by artists I like, my sketches. Almost always in the studio, there has been a creative mess, even if at the beginning there is order during the work I manage to create a mess... and then often in the background the surrounding works appear, then I started to compose them specifically, and over time the theme of the studio being predominant, many works have picture in picture."

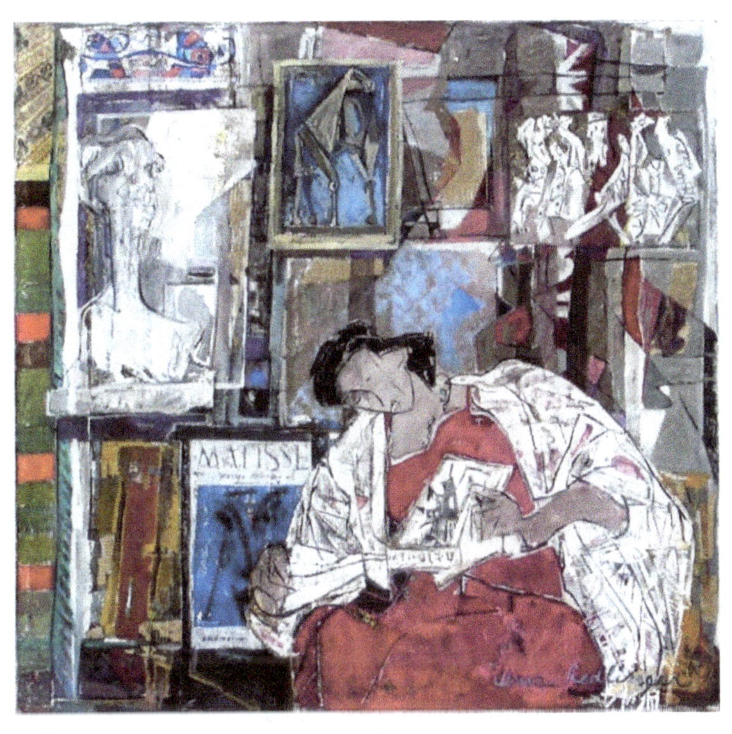

Model in studio 3, 2006, 137 × 130 cm

Discussion

"LR - Alma is a post-impressionist. I think she learned a lot from the Impressionists and more from nature. In recent years Pica has been working more in the studio. In Pica's painting, there is a lot of music, musicality of painting and music in painting... and a leaning towards ballet. Pica accompanies herself with music as she works, perhaps this explains her many paintings with a musical theme.

Daria

We used to watch TV shows together on TVR Cultural, there were many documentaries about painters' lives, their work, and exhibitions in the country and the world. We miss this program. For my mother, all these documentaries are impulses for her work.

I have always admired Petraşcu, Pallady, Luchian, Tonitza, and Iser, and I started to list them somewhat randomly, but the list is very long, perhaps even endless if it reaches the young people of today. And of course, I have to start with Maxy, the one I started with.

The Zambaccian Museum has been reorganized and now the French works in its collection are on display. There are some works thereby Delacroix, Cézanne, Picasso, Matisse, and others that I like. Influences as I told you, come through assimilation, I like, or admire something, I look in my memory and even in albums, and it probably happens that inspiration filters the things I have seen and appropriated.

Of the classics I love the great anonymous ones of the past centuries, and Rembrandt, Brueghel, Gauguin, the Impressionists, Braque, Picasso, Rouault, Matisse, Moore, and the list is just beginning again. I love them for what they created, but also for what they let me take up, to appropriate, determining me in front of paper and canvas, outside schools and currents, but together with them, as a repository of everything they let me feel, understand, express. It has been a tremendous pleasure to wander through the museums of the world, a constant joy to paint, to draw, to build."

Exhibition with works from the collection of Florica and Vasile Petrovici

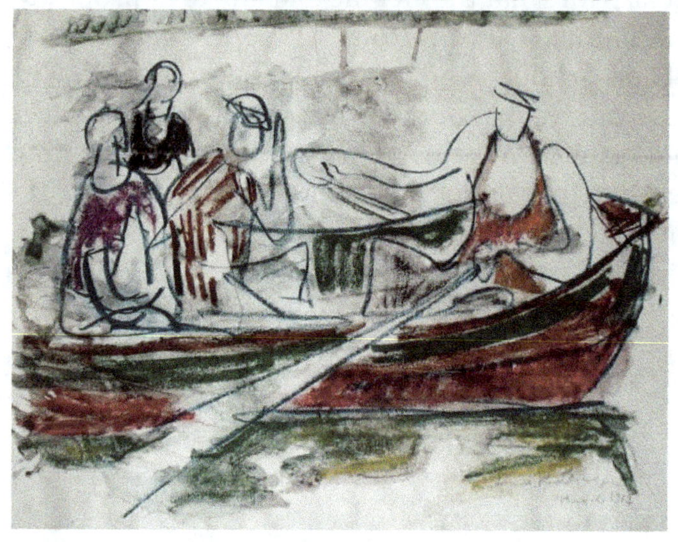

Braila, 1977, colored pencils/paper, 30 × 43 cm

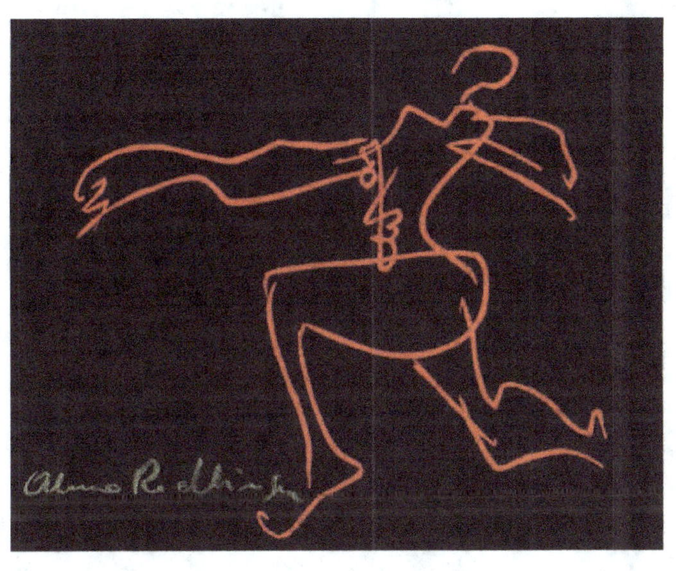

Dance, etching, 20,3 × 25,5 cm

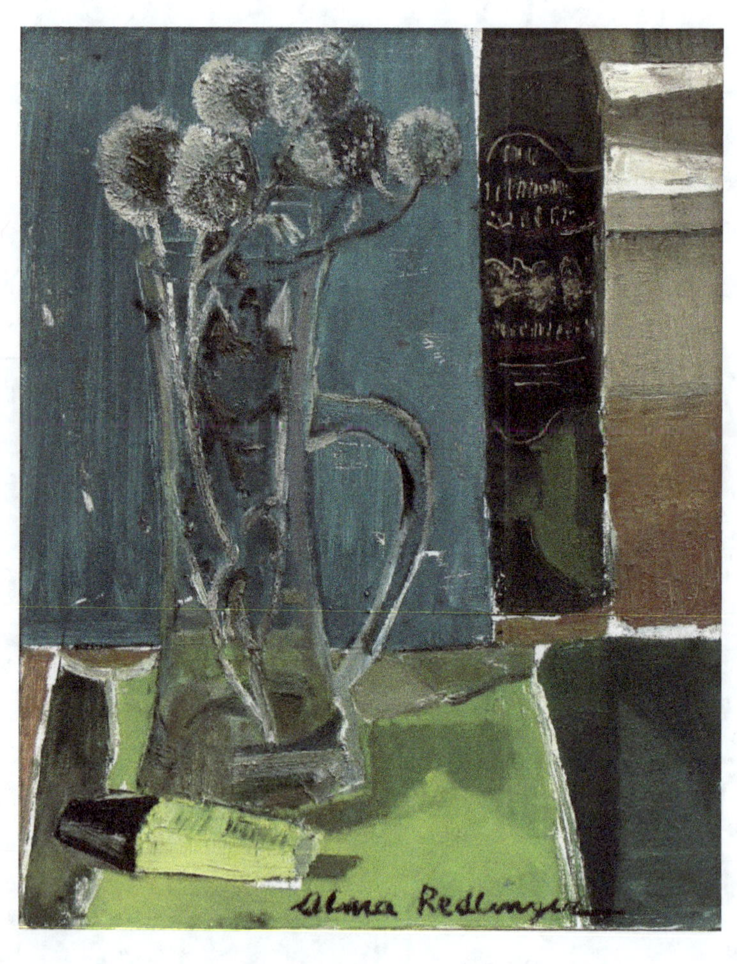

Thorns, 2005, 41 × 33 cm

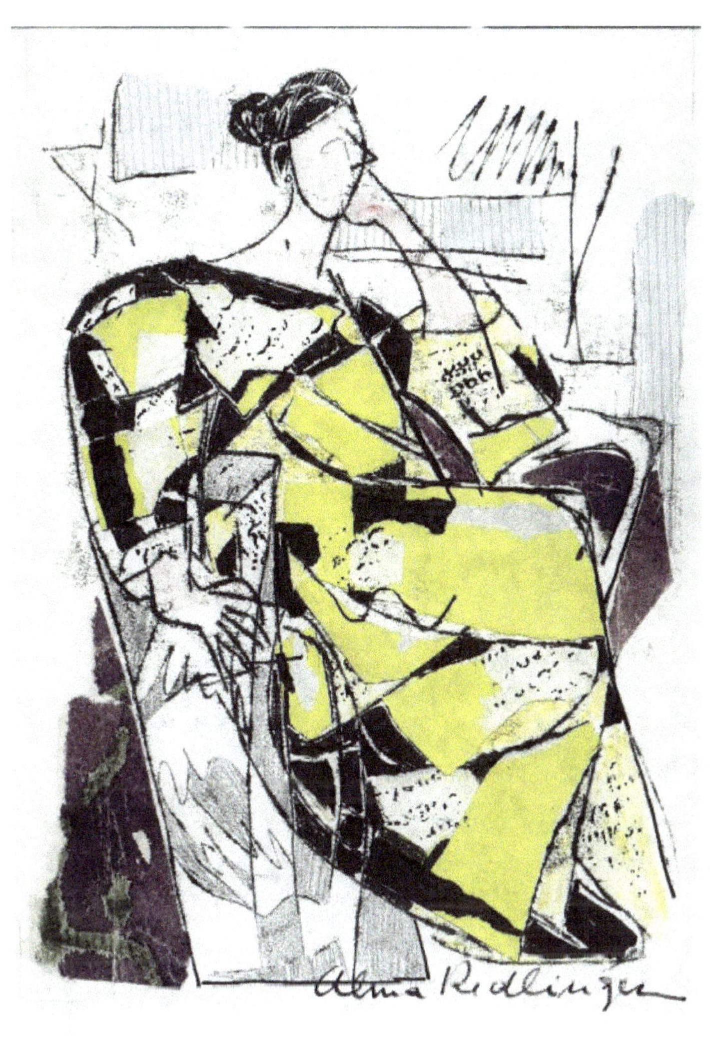

Portrait I, 2001, mixed media, 30 × 21 cm

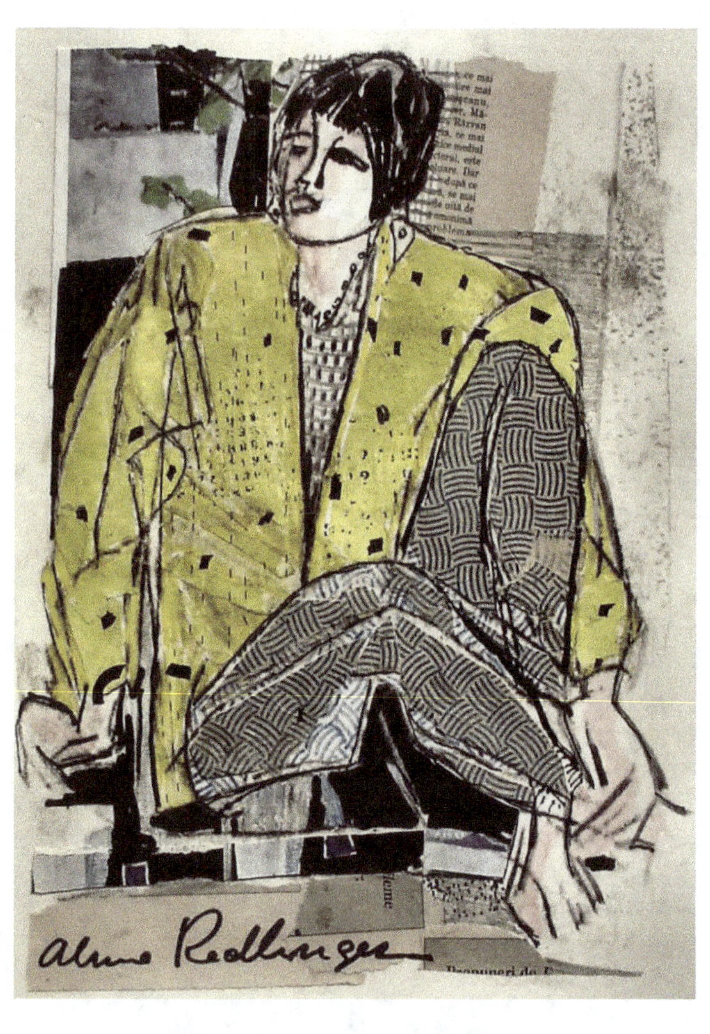

Girl in Yellow, 2001, mixed media, 29 × 19 cm

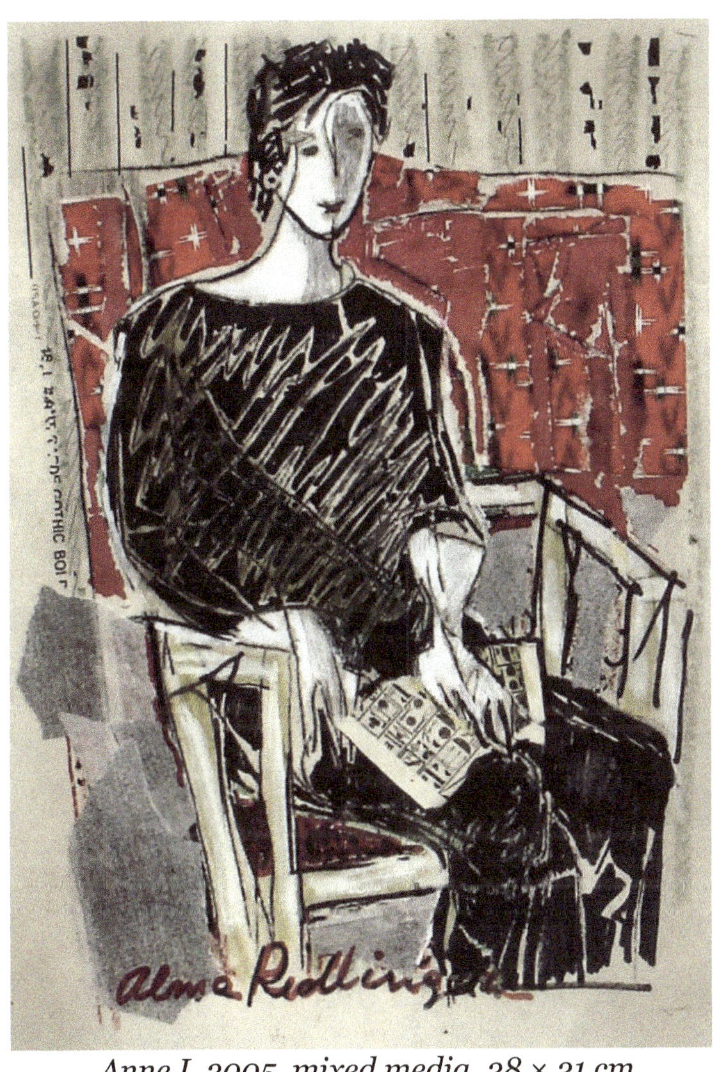

Anne I, 2005, mixed media, 28 × 21 cm

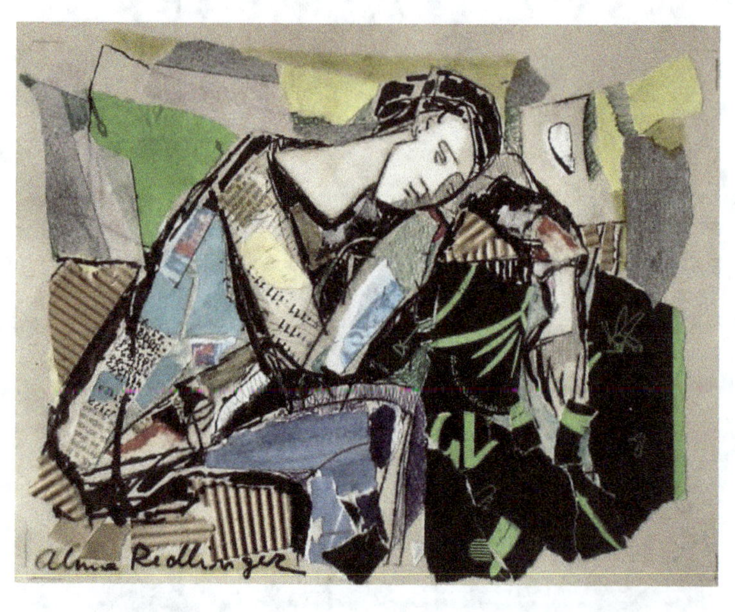

Anne II, 2005, mixed media, 21 × 29 cm

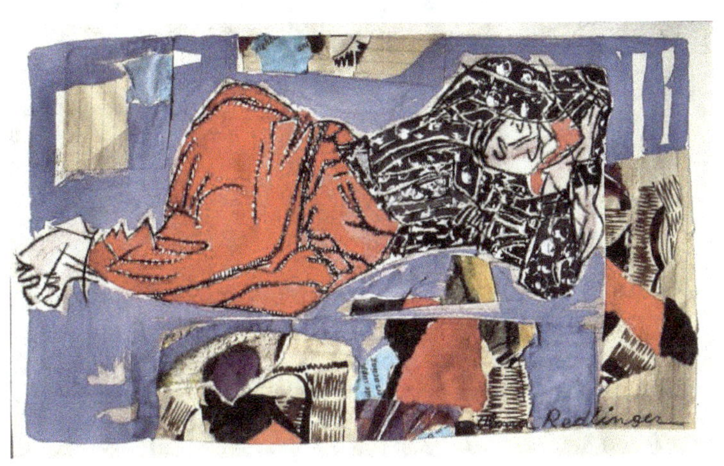

Turkish Girl, 2001, mixed media, 19 × 30 cm

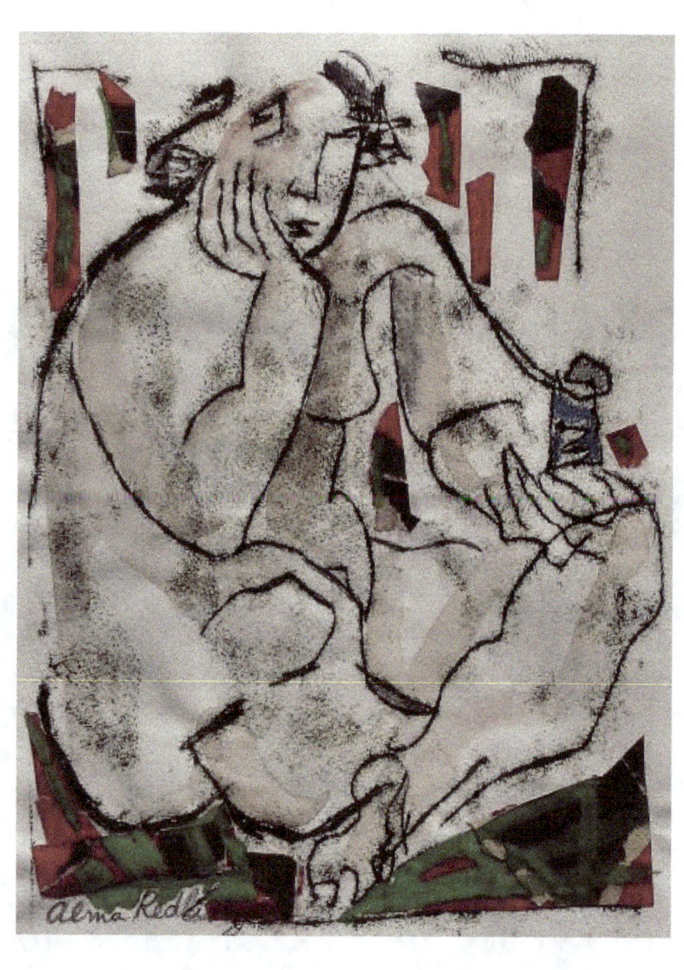

Nude, 2005, mixed media, 27 × 20 cm

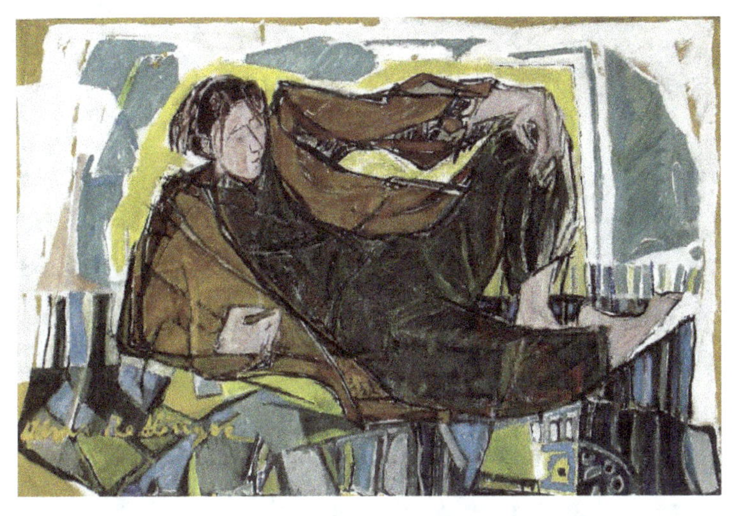

Woman in Green, 1998, 54 × 81 cm

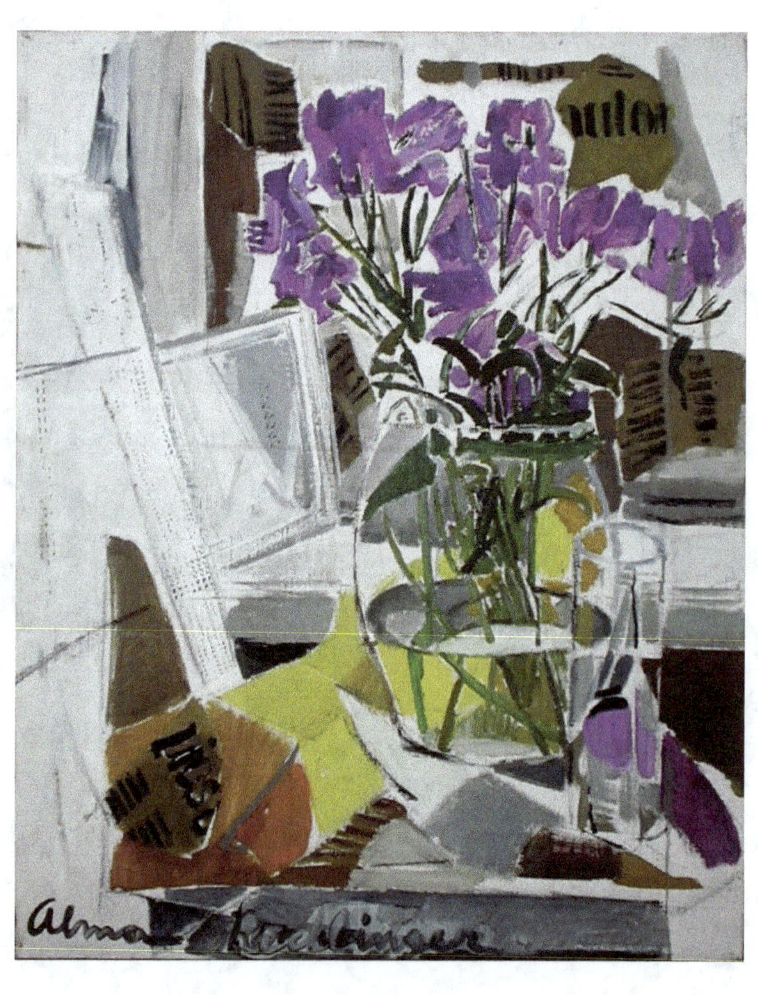

Purple Flowers, 1999, 60 × 50 cm

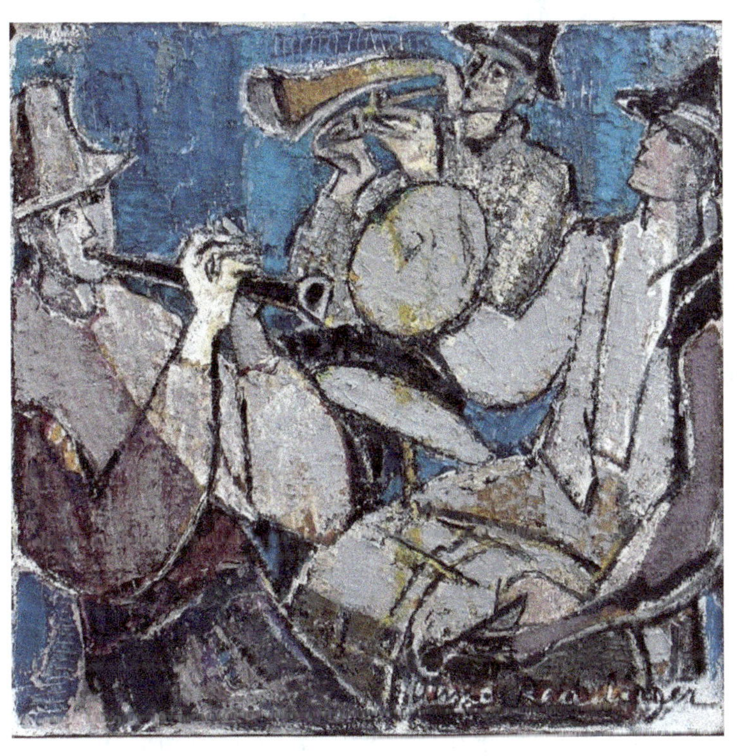

Taraf, 2013, 47 × 50 cm

Exhibition of works from the Redlinger family collection

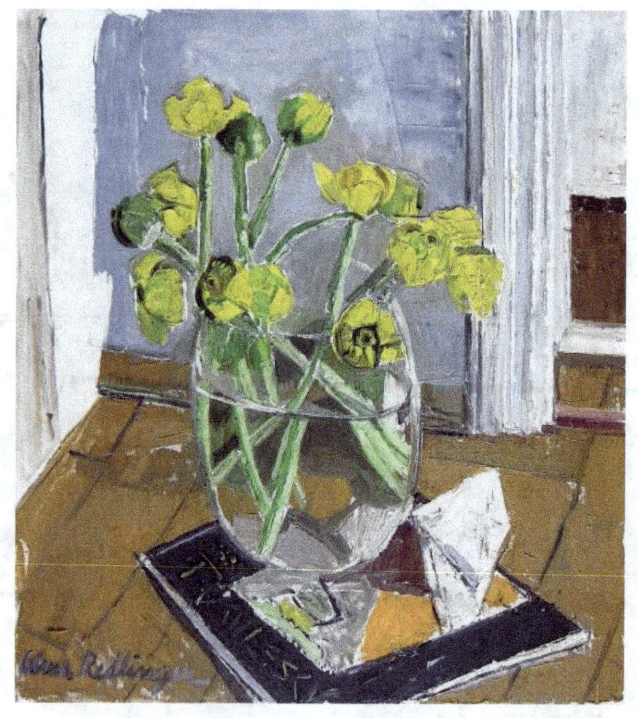

Yellow water lilies with Țuculescu album,
2012, 60 × 55 cm

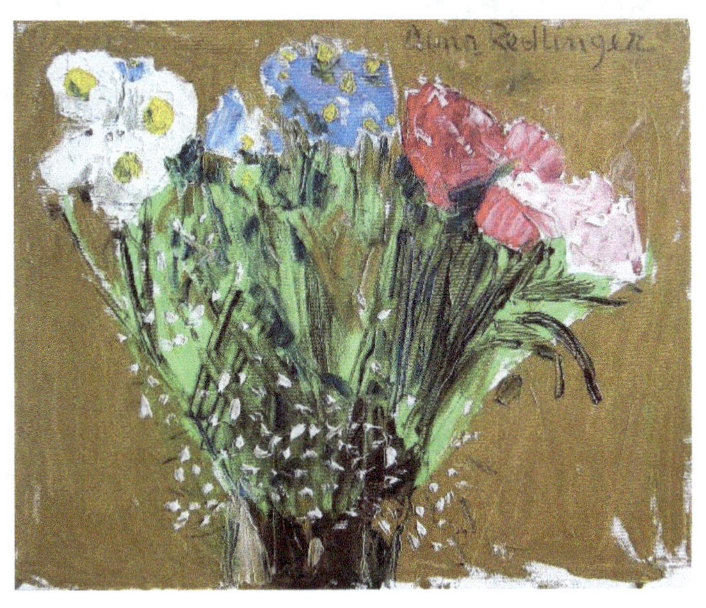

Island of Flowers, 2015,   40 × 50 cm

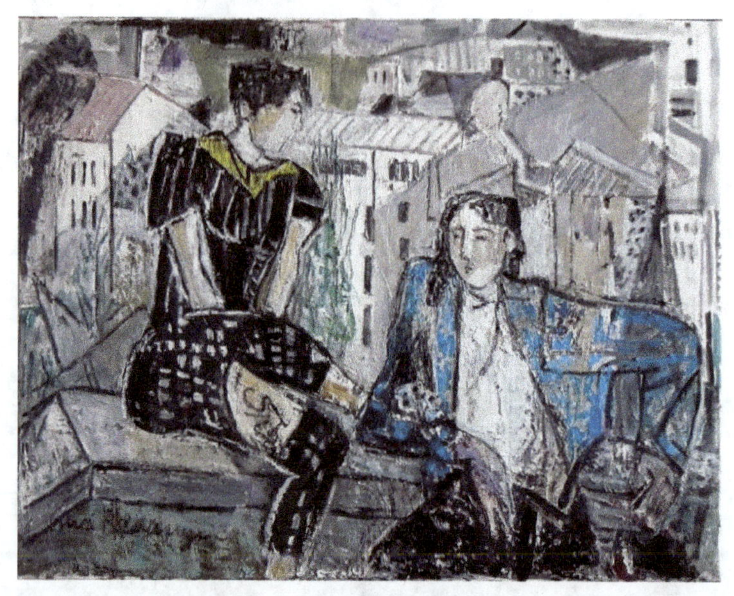

*Balcony on the seventh floor, guest on the balcony,
2013, 50 × 65 cm*

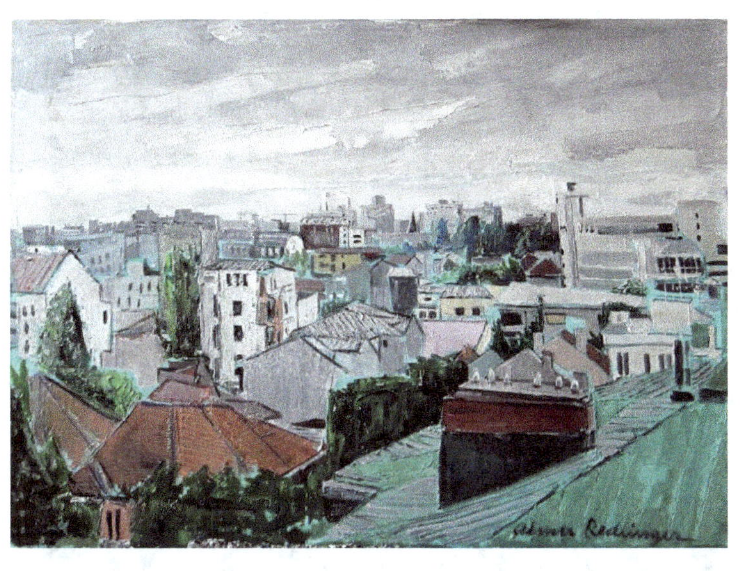

Bucharest before the storm, 2012, 70 × 100 cm

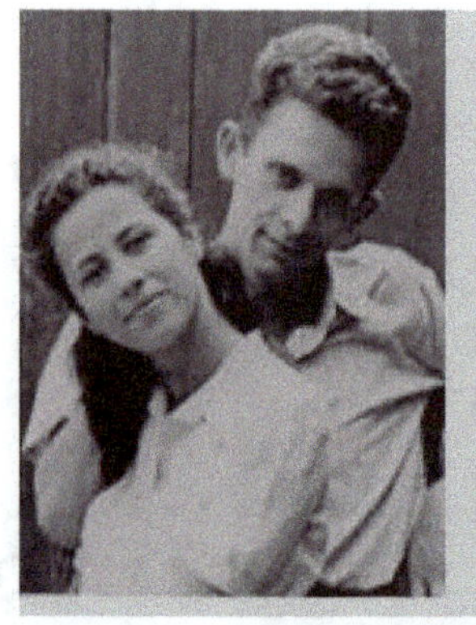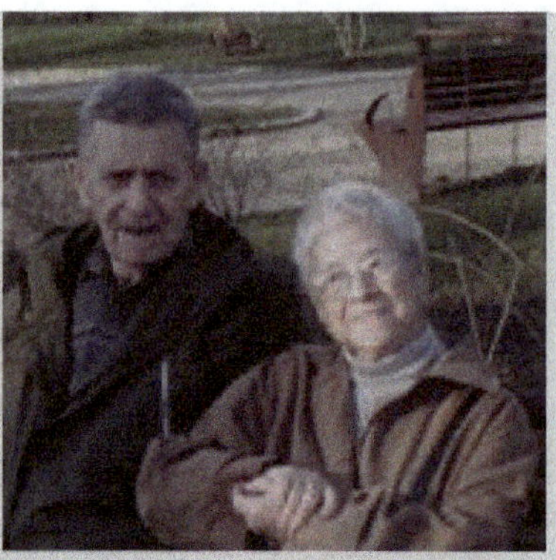

Alma (1924-2017) and Ladislau Redlinger (1921-2018), a life of love together, 1940 to 2017

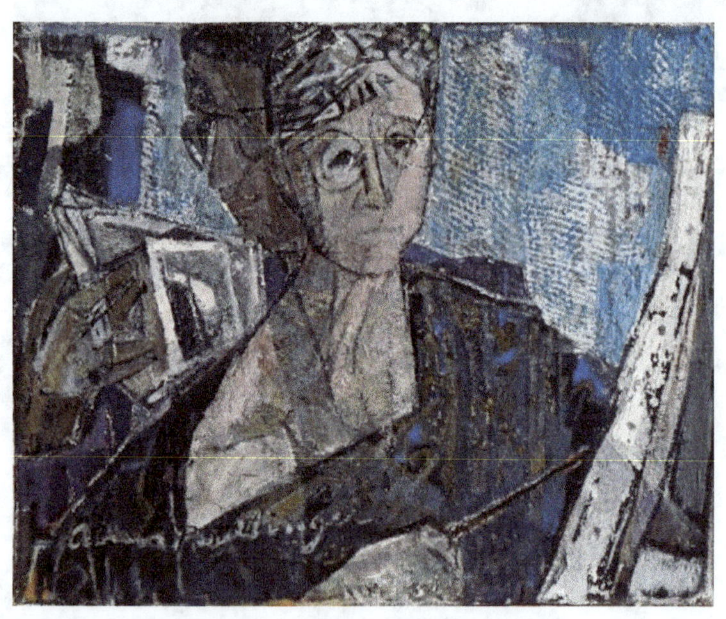

Double portrait, in front of the easel, 2006,
43 × 54 cm

The Royal Family of Romania

was saddened to learn of the passing of the artist Alma Redlinger at the venerable age of 93. Alma Redlinger was part of the generation that bridged the gap between inter-war and contemporary painting. Her art has been recognized since 1945 with the Anastase Simu Prize.

"Whoever steps into the rooms of Alma Redlinger's exhibition is fascinated from the first moment by the certainty, vigor, and authority of this painter's expression", said the art critic Radu Ionescu about her in 1994.

On 11 May 2011, His Majesty the King conferred the Royal Decoration Nihil Sine Deo on Alma Redlinger, "for her entire creative activity, carried out over several decades, in the course of which she has maintained her skill, talent, and vigor, despite the often harsh social, economic and political conditions she has suffered. For his presence in artistic life, dignified and constant, and for the fact that he did not renounce to serve the perennial values of art, reflecting the realities and ideals of society".

May he rest in peace!

Other Works

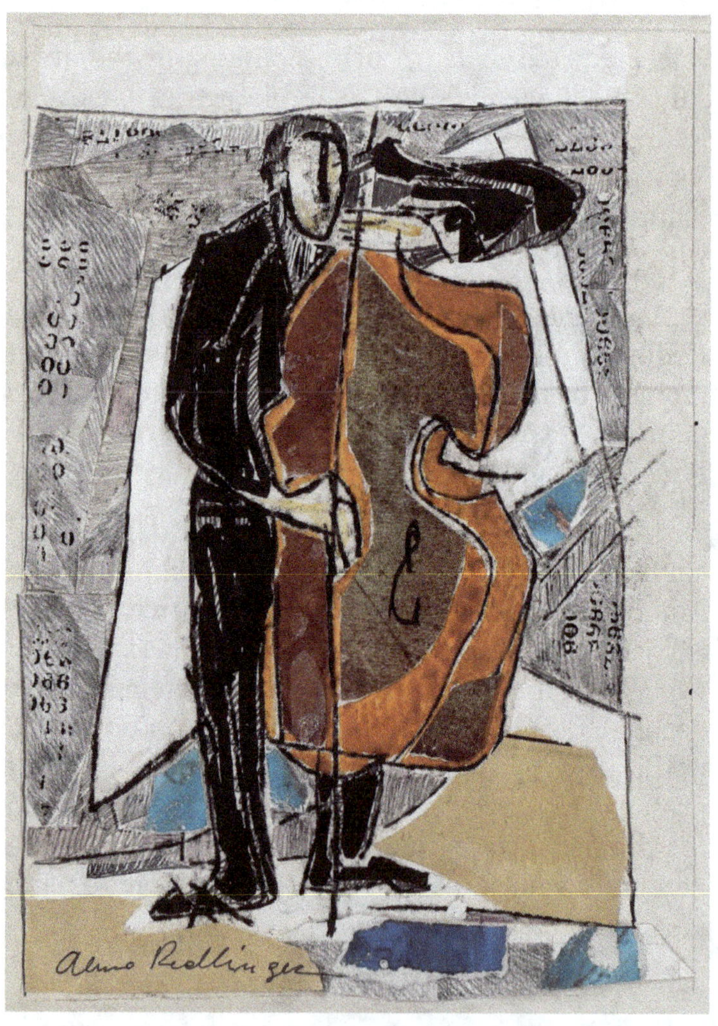

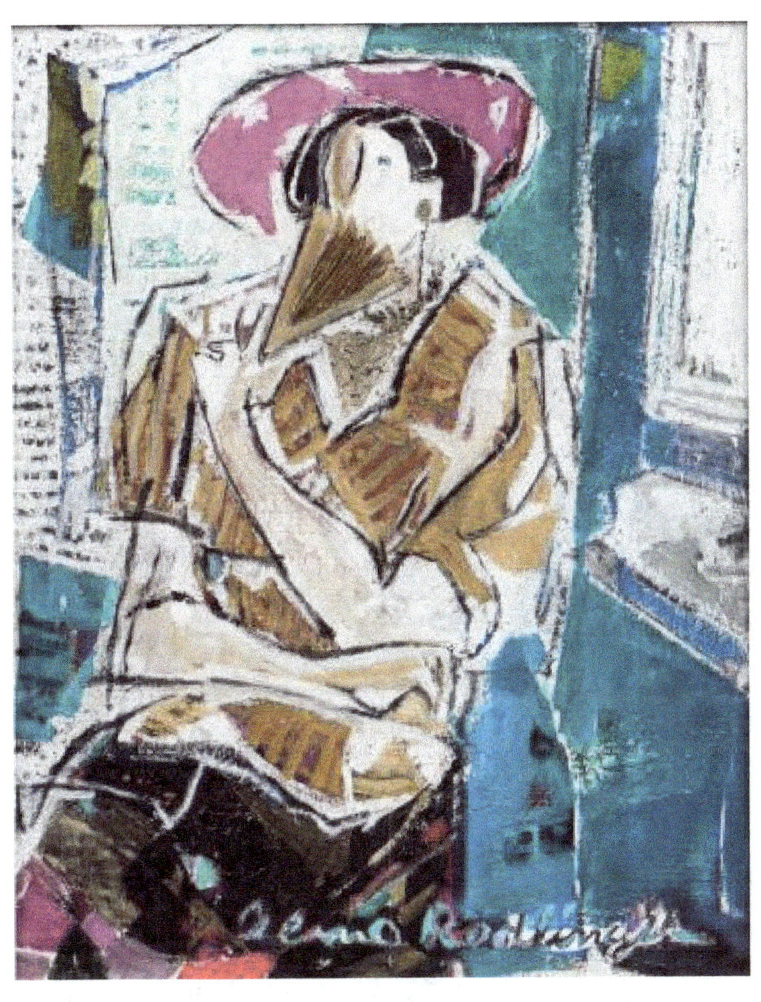

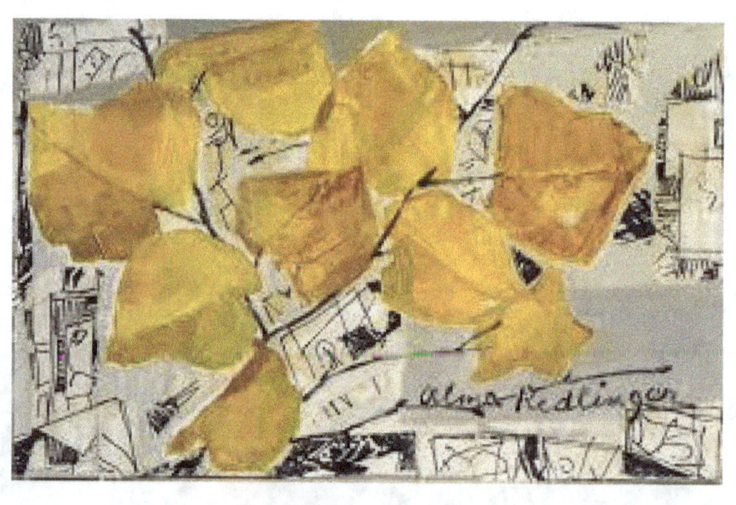

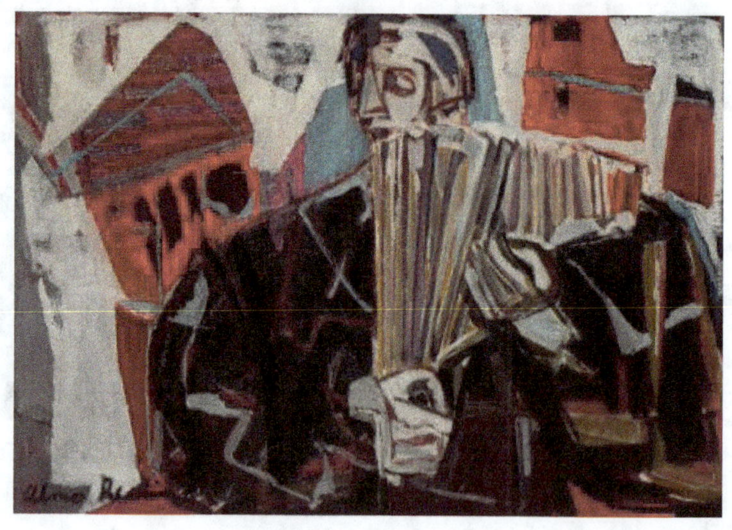

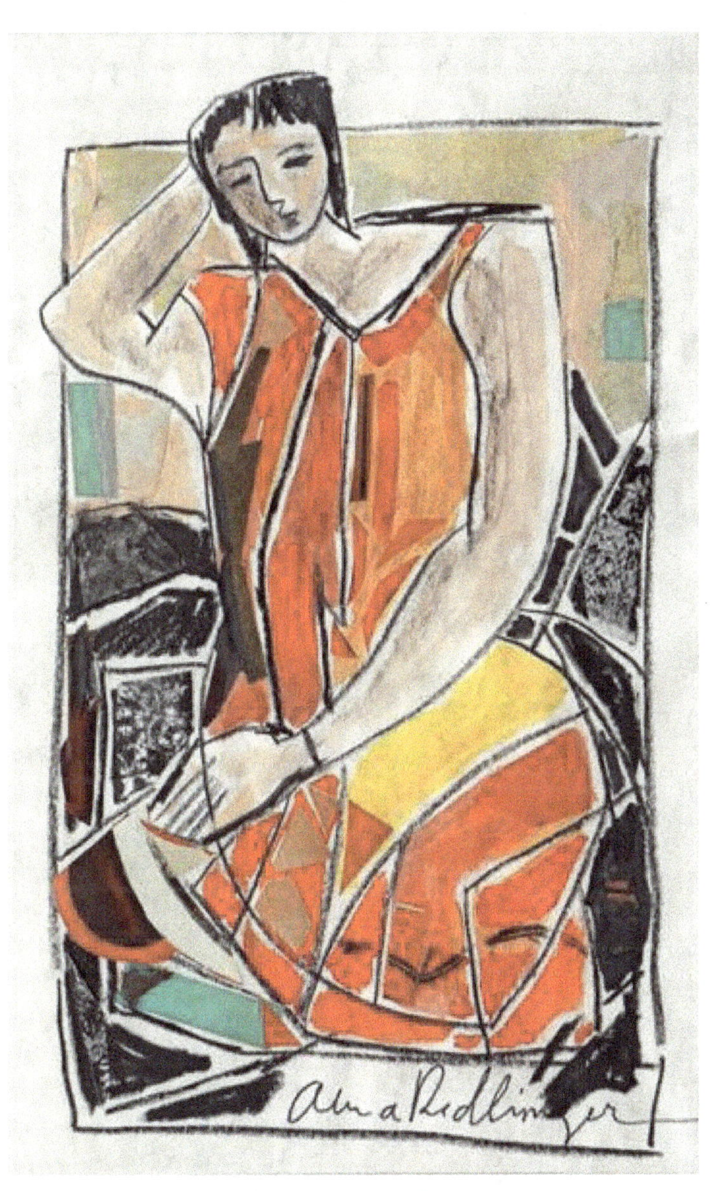

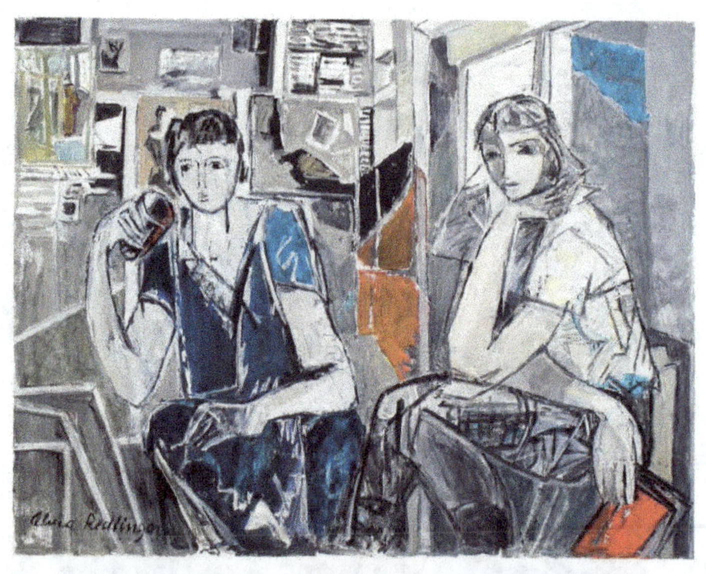

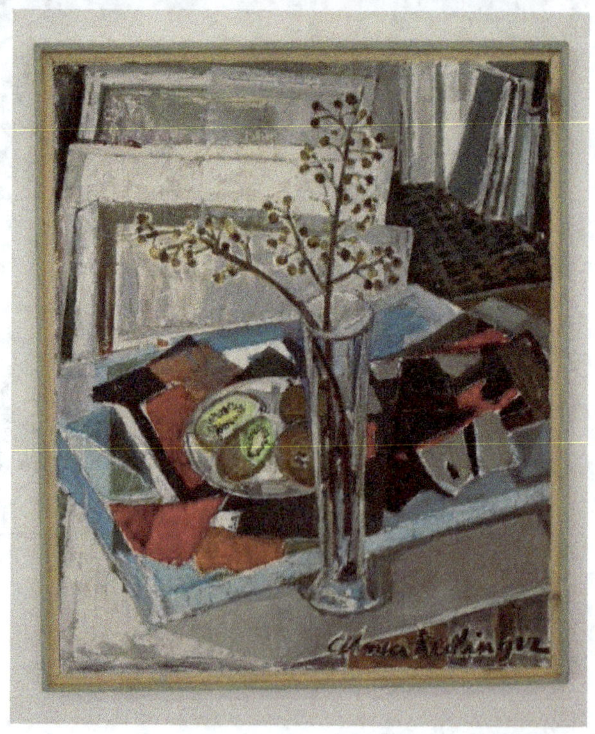

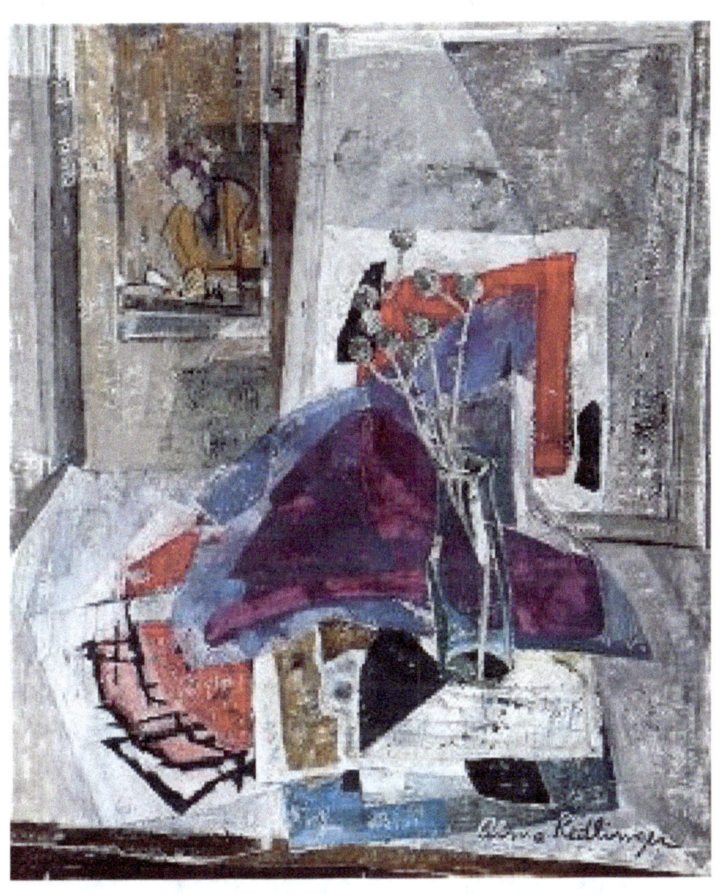

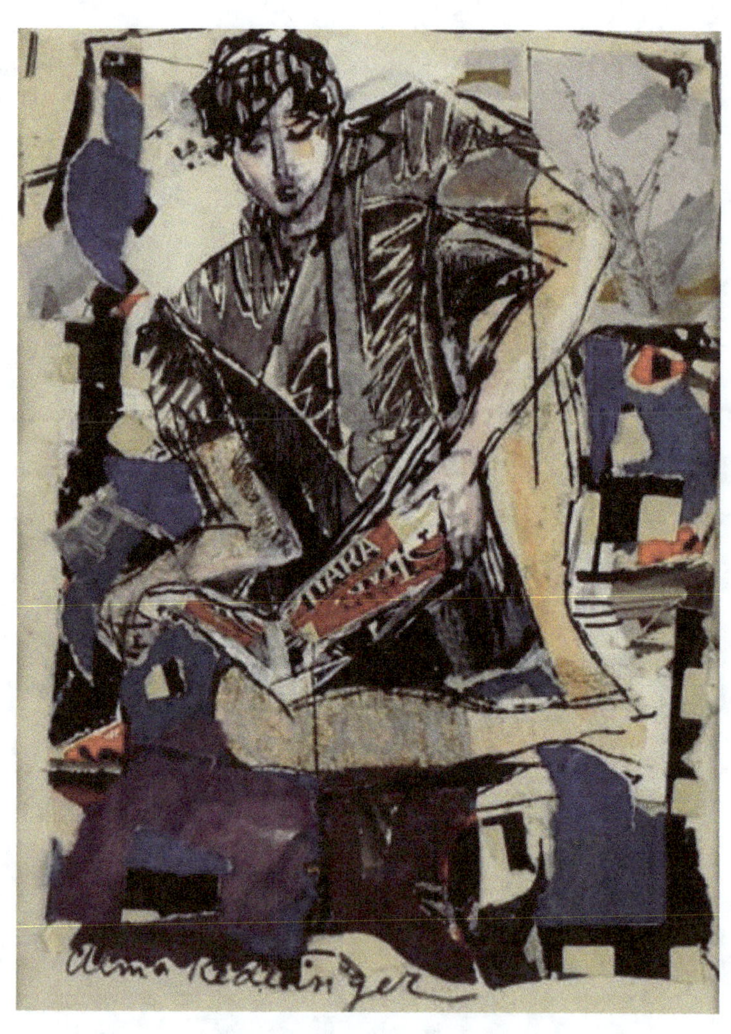

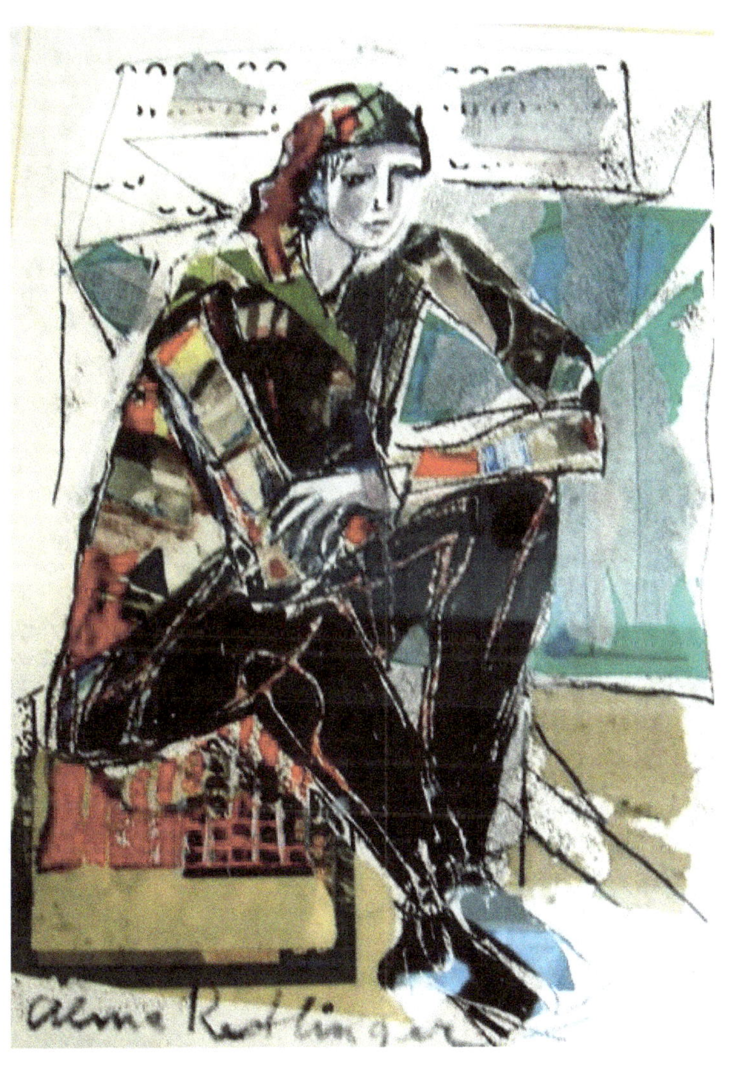

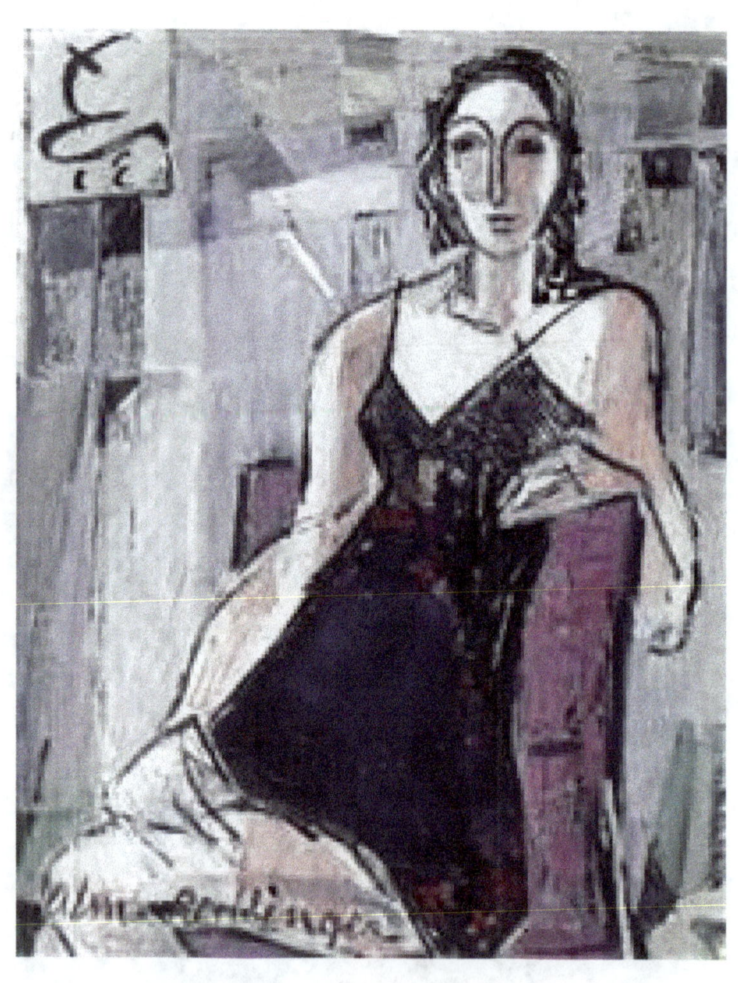

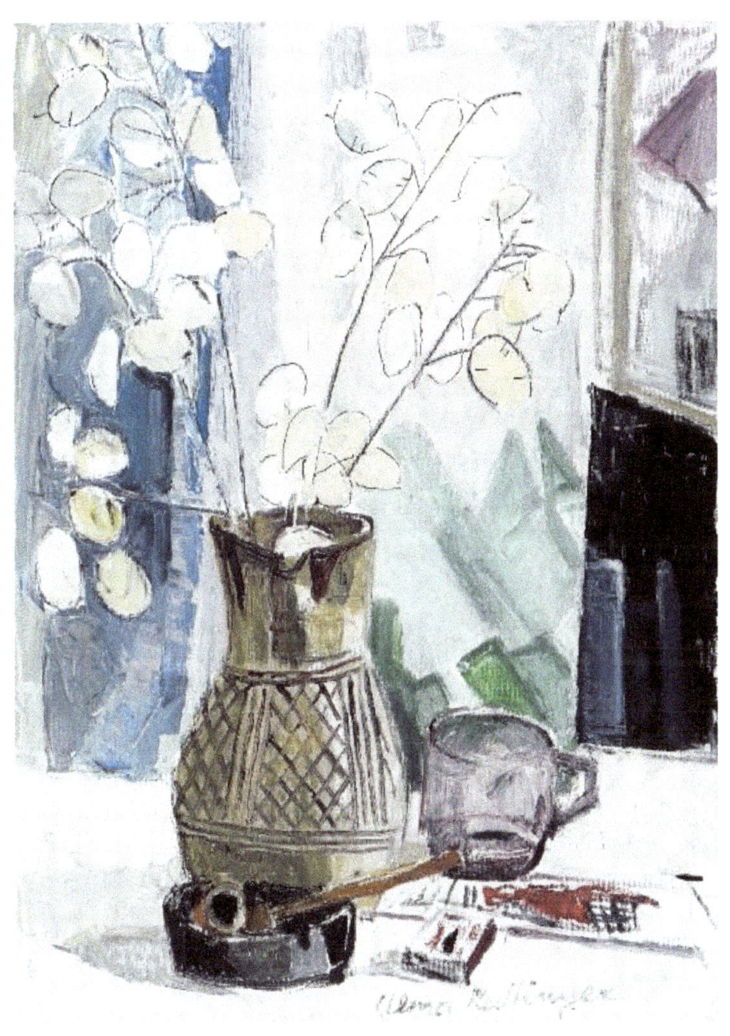

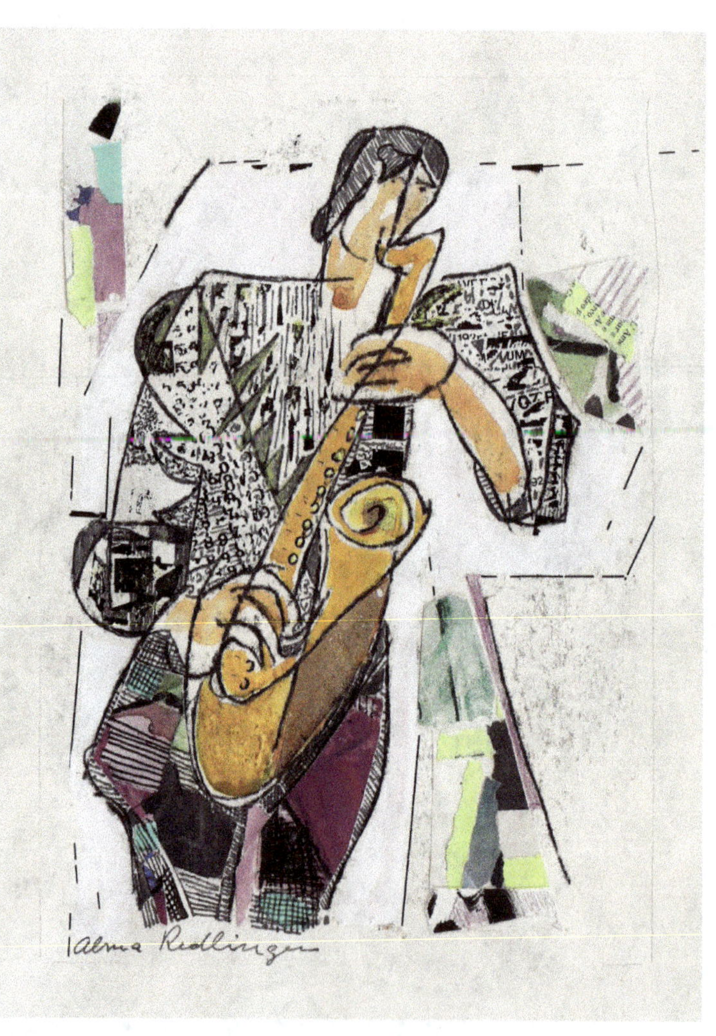

alma Redlinger

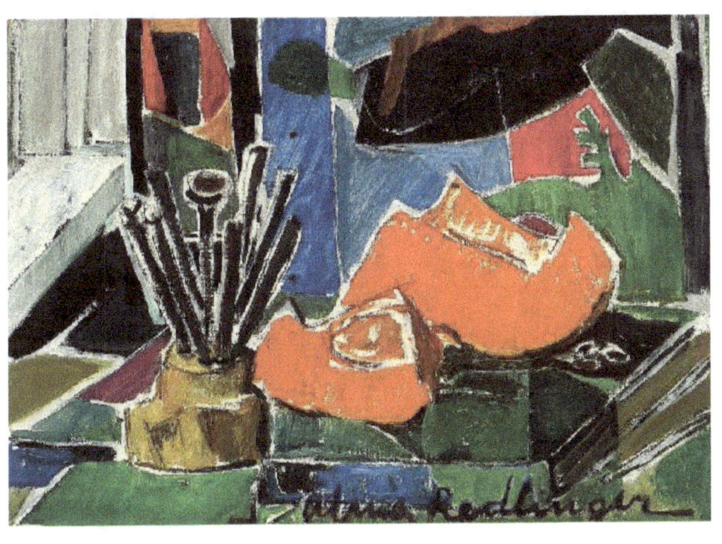

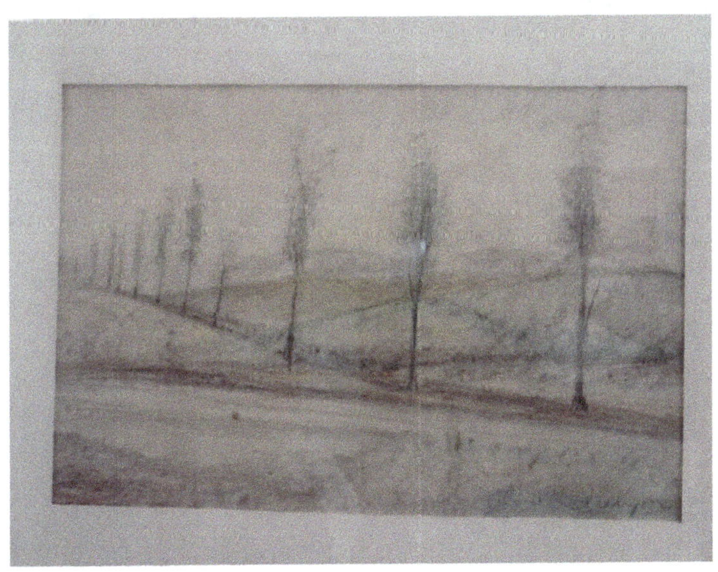

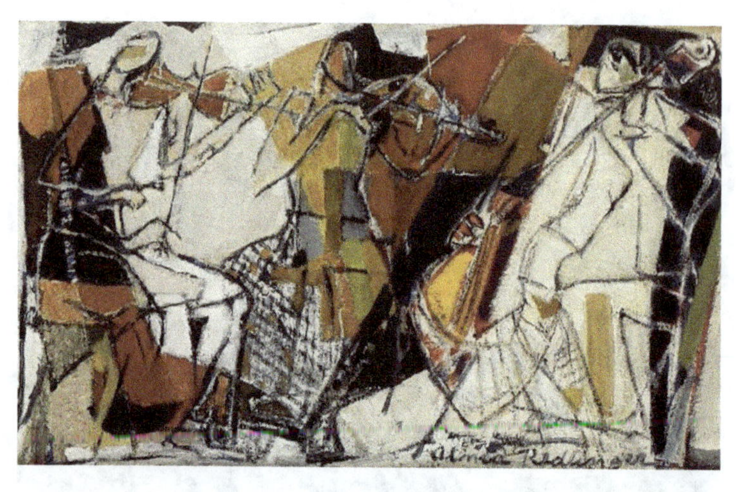

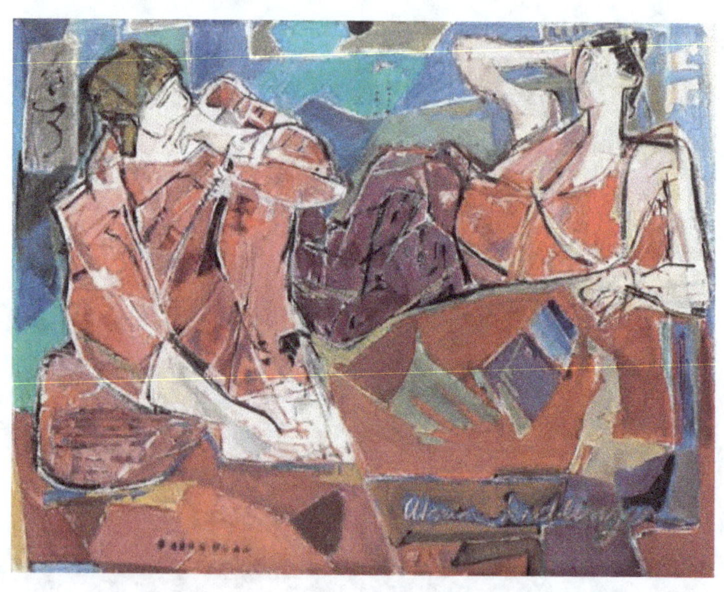

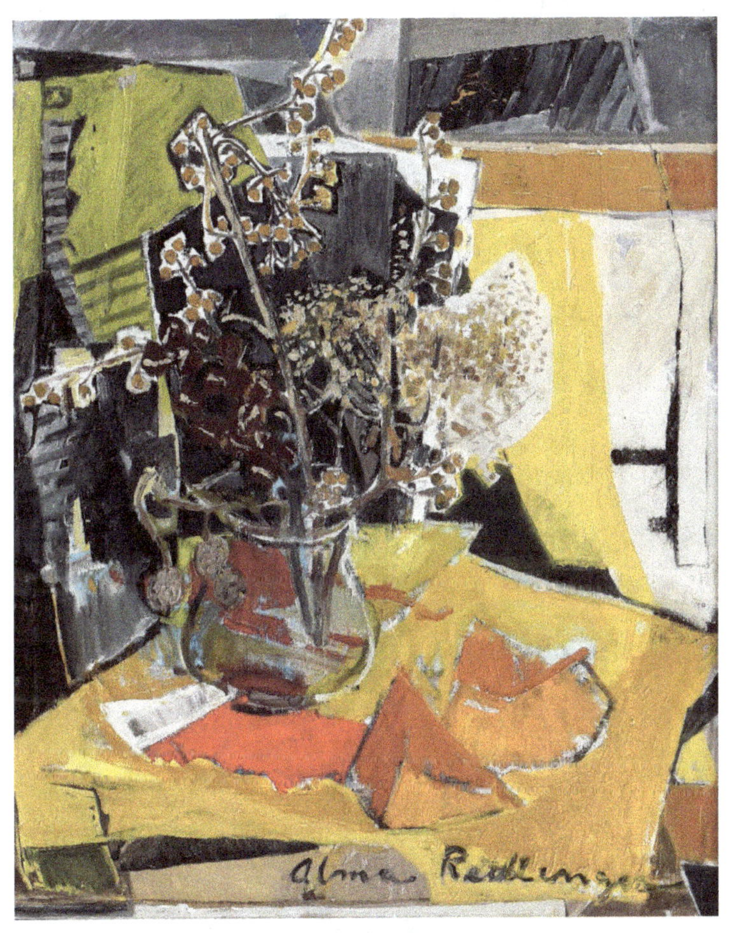

alma Redlinger

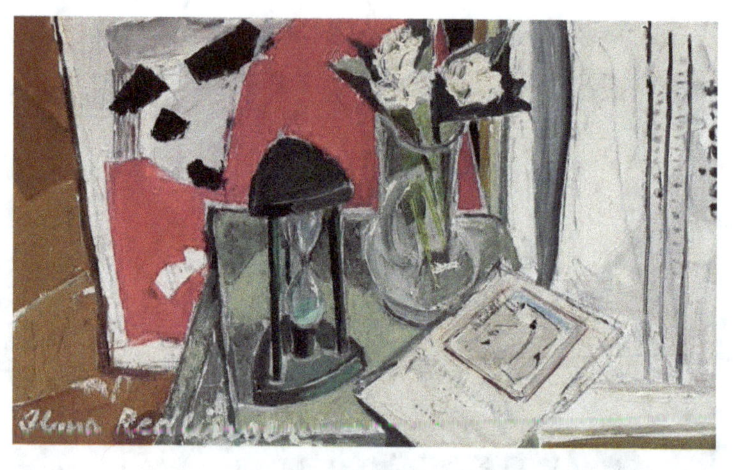

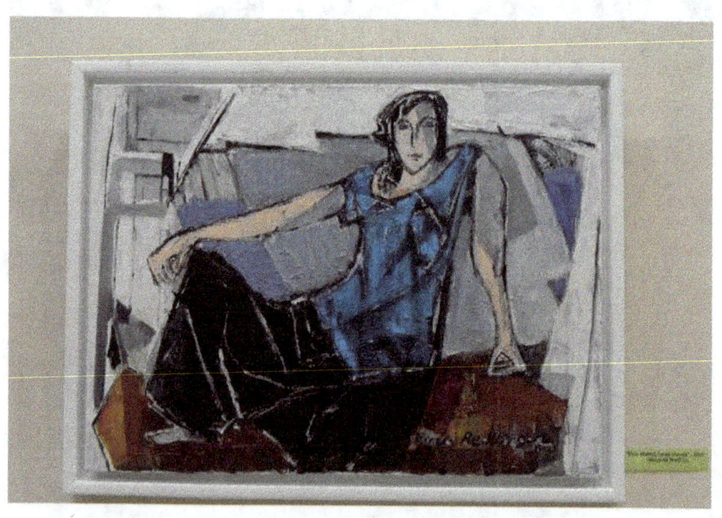

Appreciation

Adrian Buga

Because beauty springs from within and because there are factors that contribute to its birth, one must also intuit the effect of family in the creative process of Alma Redlinger. Alma Redlinger's strong, vigorous painting is an independent work.

She has found in the souls of those around her the secret of that communicable charm in which her vision acquires the plasticity and warmth of life. The emphasis falls firmly on this internal factor. Alma's artistic emotion can be found in the thoughts of Van Gogh who wrote, inspired by a daring intention: "All the love I feel for this man I must paint on my canvas".

For the first time, a painter had set out to paint his love.

I have the feeling that Alma Redlinger keeps in her pocket a secret love note that only she is allowed to look at and feel. From time to time, she reaches out and touches it only from the outside. I don't know what is written in it, but perhaps on this note, are written the names of her husband, daughters, granddaughters, and heirs.

This booklet is a modest

IN MEMORIAM dedicated to the painter ALMA REDLINGER on the 100th anniversary of her birth.

I argue that Alma's art and work are little known in Israel compared to other Jewish painters of Romanian origin. Following the path of her art, we discover a natural, dynamic, always optimistic evolution. Alma avoids Jewish subjects, the Holocaust, and the years of harmful communism, preferring a serene painting, focusing on women, flowers, still lifes, and motifs taken from the traditional Romanian landscape. As a wonderful colorist, Alma deserves wider appreciation, a presence in museums, and perhaps... retrospective exhibitions. SAGA Publishing is honored to present Alma's art to readers in the Diaspora, Israel, USA...on the occasion of Redlinger's centenary.

Special thanks to Daria Simion and the collector and author of Talking to Alma Redlinger - Vasile Petrovici.

Editor Note

www.ingramcontent.com/pod-product-compliance
Lightning Source LLC
Chambersburg PA
CBHW070032260726

48658CB00002B/606